Oriental Sex
Man[...]

HOWA[...]

*A guide to the bizarre sexual morality
of the East*

Oriental Sex Manners

HOWARD LEVY

*A guide to the bizarre sexual morality
of the East*

ORIENTAL SEX MANNERS

Oriental Sex Manners

Howard S. Levy

NEW ENGLISH LIBRARY
TIMES MIRROR

This book is dedicated to Max and Rae Faerber, the booksellers and publishers who have assisted me and encouraged me throughout my writing career.

NEL Books are published by
New English Library Limited from Barnard's Inn, Holborn, London E.C.1.
Made and printed in Great Britain by Hunt Barnard Printing Ltd., Aylesbury, Bucks.

450010821

Contents

Appendices: Sex and Today's Japan

Introduction

I chose the title deliberately, placing sex before love, for it seems to me that with the Japanese the search for sexual pleasure is paramount and the love that may accompany this search of secondary concern. Japan never had its equivalent of the Western crusades, with troubadours exalting woman on a pedestal as the inexpressibly grand and unattainable; the Japanese male has kept woman down to earth and in easy reach of his beck and call. To exalt or idealise her was considered unmanly, unbecoming, and un-Japanese. She could be educated in one of two ways, the way of the housewife or the way of the whore. The housewife-to-be was taught to be home oriented and submissive to the male, complying with the so-called 'Three Obediences' to father, husband, and son, while the whore was given rigorous training in how to cater to male sexuality and egotism through keen awareness of his needs and an inculcated desire to please. I refer to these traditions in the past tense, for in modern Japan they are undergoing a rapid and continuous transformation. Woman's status has markedly improved in the decades since the war ended in 1945, and in the post-war era she has moved out of the confines of the home, much more socially involved and much less fettered.

Since I read modern Japanese with facility, I was able to secure my information from a wide range of Japanese books, monographs, and magazine articles. Japan is the only society in Asia which is easily accessible because it lacks the censorship of the heavy-handed one-party dictatorship, and the mass circulation weeklies and journals pay a lot of attention to relations of the sexes and to significant trends. I noted some of these studies in an earlier annotated bibliography,* and here I've appended a few essay summaries of magazine articles, to give the reader some idea of their scope and significance. They include such diverse subjects as the virginity outlook, the effects of crowded conditions on newlyweds, arranged marriages vs. love marriages, sex sensitivity zones of Japanese women, and Japanese rules for girl-watching. These studies are merely a sample of the information on sex and

*See *The Tao of Sex*, second edition, especially pages 237–259.

love which pours forth from the Japanese media, awaiting translation and interpretation by qualified investigators.

I made a continued effort to double-check the validity of my information and took advantage of visits to Japan in the summer of 1970 and the early winter of 1971 by consulting with local authorities on specific problems. Apart from the appendices, my book consists of a series of essays. In the first essay, I describe how the Japanese woman has been physically evolving in the past hundred years, generally becoming taller and more slender, sinewy and less fat. She now spends less time squatting on the straw mats called *tatami* and more time sitting on chairs. The result? Her legs are getting more shapely, something I noticed increasingly during my eight years in Japan (1961-1969). The corpulent legs that look like a Japan type of radish, which the Japanese derisively call 'radish legs' (*daikon ashi*), are becoming a vestige of the past. (If you haven't been in Japan since the late forties or early fifties, go back now and take another look at those shapely young Japanese legs – you're bound to be pleasantly surprised.) My first essay is followed by a recorded conversation that I had just before leaving Japan, with Dr Akira Ishihara, a renowned Japanese physician-historian-sexologist. We talked informally about Japanese and Western sex practices, trying to show where they're similar and where they differ. Dr Ishihara freely admits that Japan is adopting Western ways, but he thinks it will take another thirty years for Japanese women to assume the prerogatives (and the hang-ups?) of Western females.

With the third essay we delve into Japanese history, focusing on the fact that the ancients more or less married as they pleased. Eligible Japanese bachelors and single women emulated the ancient Chinese, meeting on festival days in spring and autumn. They chose their mates through special song competitions and spurred themselves on sexually with wine, merriment, and selective fun and games. They must have been as leery about marital mishaps as we are, for they went in for trial marriages in which the male paid a prolonged visit to the house of his intended bride. Incidentally, clandestine arrangements somewhat like these are made in remote northern districts of Japan to the present day, though of course they are officially forbidden.

Some Japanese villages considered girls at puberty to be communal property, to be possessed in common by the village youths. And a girl remained a joint possession until she married one of the group. In a male-based society, this custom proved hard to eradicate, persisting in certain areas till the start of the twentieth century. Premarital sex therefore was an irrepressible aspect of village life. But while the Japanese went in for early sex, for centuries they held an awesome view of female virginity, equating it with the divine to such a degree that holy priests were directed to deflorate virgins as a part of their religious duties. In my readings I was reminded again and again of how the Japanese inextricably coupled sex and religion, placing the altar and the whorehouse in meaningful proximity. Even today, major religious festivals are held periodically at ex-whorehouse shrines.

The early Japanese were admirably free of sexual hang-ups, for to them sex was a natural and enjoyable function with no connotation of sin. Japan's Adam and Eve, Izanagi and Izanami, looked at their sexual organs and came to the conclusion that excess and lack should be joined together. And so they were, with no concept of wrong-doing involved. Prudery about sex didn't take hold until the religious do-gooders came on the scene. To Buddhist and Confucian doctrinaires Eros was suspect, but despite their warnings and injunctions a natural way of looking at sex permeated all social classes. Confucian theorists took their cue from the double-standard Chinese and advocated chastity for the woman, concubines for the men. Of course Mencius had said that it was unfilial not to have progeny, but much of the later rationalisations must have developed around a sexual base. We cannot help but note that, as in China, men (but never women!) could get divorced for the most trivial of reasons. Widows were urged to live without sex, and those who did so were posthumously honoured. The real tragedies must have occurred with those child brides whose mates-to-be died in adolescence. Varying by era, but especially characteristic of military rule, women of important clans were forced into political marriages, regardless of their feelings.

The sex lives of Japan's feudal rulers, referred to as *shogun*, are presented in enough detail to clarify what seem to us today to be the bizarre arrangements of the *shogun's* boudoir. In Tokugawa Japan (1603–1867) there was keen awareness of the political intrigue potential of bewitching harem favourites, so a careful watch was kept on boudoir ladies to keep them from extracting political favours or engaging in political intrigues. The *shogun* enjoyed easy sex with all, but carefree private sex only with female bath attendants, and in later era even hot bath dalliance was officially discouraged. Feudal lords called *diamyo* had shogun-like harems, but on a smaller scale.

Our essay on prostitution reinforces the age-old association of

9

religion and sex, with shamanesses servicing the gods and their priestly representatives. The shamaness who left palace environs and went back home often made her living there by selling her charms to the highest bidder. The whore or the woman spurned might spend her remaining years in a nunnery, reminded of the evanescence of emotional involvements in the mundane realm. In Japan this process of worldly detachment was at one time reversed, with 'singing nuns' lining the roads in anticipation of patronage by well-heeled tourists.

The Japanese recognised Eros and tried to confine it within specified brothel areas. The most famous whorehouses, called The Yoshiwara, flourished for three centuries until the spring of 1958, when they were officially outlawed. For three centuries these houses were tolerated, but only under strict government regulation, the concept being one of controlling prostitution by confining it in scope and location. And even today the major entertainment centres are kept within easy distance of the local police-box. With the Meiji Restoration of 1868 and the large-scale entry of Westerners, the Japanese became sensitive to observance and criticism by outsiders, with condemnation of the whorehouse phenomenon by morality-minded foreigners playing a role in the weakening of the institution and its formal abolition. But, like many things in the East, the whore survives in another guise. She may be a bar-girl, a hostess, a street-walker (though increasingly rare), or even as a so-called Turkish bath attendant. The latter, a centuries old phenomenon in modern form, thrives in amusement centres in the large cities, offering a variety of comforts and services.

In terms of sexuality, we might describe the East as a civilisation complex whose ideology allowed man to exploit his sadistic tendencies at the expense of a masochistically indoctrinated female. Woman was formally instructed to submit and obey, and her endurance of male abuse was officially tolerated if not encouraged. The history of Japanese tortures supports this contention, for women were subjected to male maltreatment and humiliation in ways inconceivable to Western minds. The adulteress and the wayward whore were special prey for male sadists.

I hope that my book provides accurate information for anyone interested in the subject of sex, love, and the Japanese; the intention is to inform and to elucidate. No one today will deny that sex is an integral part of human life, East or West, worthy of proper understanding and evaluation. We still have, unfortunately, many histories of China and Japan which either delicately detour around sexual themes or blithely ignore them. The impartial observer cannot fail to note with surprise that the sexual 'bamboo curtain' is so rarely lowered. Japan, being a relatively open society, offers excellent possibilities for investigation and eventual contrast and comparison with other industralised societies. We can look forward to the day when the thrust of Western scholarship on Asia moves away from irrelevance and obscurity and in the direction of grappling directly with problems involving social concepts and ways of being. And since the sex life is a part of the larger life, its study can provide us with one of the major keys to understanding the inner fabric of Asian societies.

I. Japanese Women Then and Now

The past hundred years have witnessed a series of dramatic and revolutionary changes in Japanese society, and equally dramatic have been the changes effected in Japanese body build and proportions. This has been especially true of the Japanese woman; in what ways has she changed and why did these changes occur?

Women in Japan are, on the average, several inches taller than they were at the turn of the century and they are growing at a quicker pace than are the men. This development was adversely affected by World War II, when food shortages were widespread, and female growth was stunted from then until the immediate post-war age. The pre-war standard of female height wasn't reached again until 1952 and it took another two years for it to be surpassed.

The significant point about this growth is that it has all taken place from the waist down! The Japanese woman compares favourably with her European and American counterparts as to the length of her trunk, with slight but not sharp differences between them. With her trunk virtually unchanged, therefore, she's put all of the additional inches into her legs. And, as photographs of nineteenth century Japanese women indicate, squat legs used to be one of her leading characteristics.

How about the size of her breasts? What changes, if any, have taken place in the bust and the area around the bust? There have been two ways of measuring the bust in Japan, one referred to as the 'under bust' (in the case of schoolgirl statistics) and the other as the 'top bust' (for beauty contestants). The bust as such is not larger, since the Japanese woman has less fatty tissue than she had a century ago, but she's become larger-boned and there has been an increase in the size of the thoracic cavity. The length of her trunk is the same but there's been a positive development in the roundness of her bust contours, with the bones that form the framework getting larger.

The most remarkable change in the proportions of the Japanese

13

women today as contrasted with the last century is in the noticeable lengthening of her legs. And, as noted above, her bust is more rounded. Besides these changes, her waist has gotten smaller and her hips have gotten higher than they used to be. Western woman historically has devoted a good deal of attention to waist reduction, but this was never an important factor for the Japanese woman because the waist as such tended to get lost within the folds of her kimono and the sash that kept it in place. The lack of concern with waist and hips is indicated by the fact that no data has yet been compiled nationwide about either. But a careful inspection of the photographs of nudes and bathing beauties dating from the late nineteenth and early twentieth centuries leads one to the reasonable conclusion that waists are indeed becoming ever more slender. One investigation carried out at a girl's school in Tokyo revealed a waist reduction of almost one inch effected from 1951 to 1961, only a ten-year period. Maybe we can call this evolution in Japan one from the waistless figure to the coke bottle shape, in which slender waists contrast with firmly shaped hips. This waist reduction is due to the gradual reduction of fat below the skin of the stomach and the development of a more sinewy body build. The waist is still a little large by Western standards, so further slenderising is anticipated.

How about the hips? Since the size of the head has remained unchanged in the past hundred years, it is hypothesised that the pelvic region has likewise remained unchanged. But with the reduction of fatty tissue the hips of Japanese women have gotten decidedly firmer and, to the interested observer, they appear trimmer than before. And the hips are moving upwards, related to a new life style which emphasises better nutrition and a more active woman who is on the go, involved in numerous sports and social activities. The slenderising of the waist, the firming of the buttocks, and the lengthening of the legs has been accompanied by a weight gain of about ten pounds, achieved over the past seven decades prior to this one. In general, the Japanese woman is developing a larger body build, though her body weight has remained the same for the past decade. But she continues to get slightly taller and smarter in appearance, less fat and more sinewy-slender than her predecessors.

In general, during Japanese history it was the warlord epochs that exalted the fleshy female and the peaceful and esthetically-oriented epochs that stressed beauty standards of delicacy, willow waists, sloping shoulders, and white skins. Woman was confined to home and directed to concentrate her energies on husband-

14

pleasing, family rearing, and domesticity. But while in the Meiji era (1868–1911) the consumptive looking female was regarded as ideal, to day the emphasis is on vibrant health and athletic vigour. To recapitulate, in the past hundred years the Japanese woman has gotten noticeably taller, with this height achieved through the legs. Her weight has increased somewhat, her head and trunk size remain unchanged, and her bust has become more rounded. Her waist has gotten more slender, and her hips are firmer and on the upwards move. What used to be known as 'radish' legs because of their rotundity have gotten much more slender, with a closer approximation now from woman to woman in leg proportions. What she's lost in stoutness she's gained in muscular development, and while her bust is no larger it is more attractively formed. These changes in physique go along with a revolutionary change in her life style. No longer quiescent or confined to the home, she is a vigorous and active social participant, perhaps not as feminine at a glance as she used to be but certainly more vibrant than ever before and imbued with a new, outer-directed sensuality. She may not be as gentle and lovable as she once was, but she's now more interested in fulfilling her own needs than she is in subordinating these needs to the waywardness of the male. No longer content to be a homebody, she's more apt now to be earning her own living and to be enjoying the economic status that places her on a more equal footing with the male. No longer always at her mother's side, she is lively and more courageous than she was in pre-war times and is becoming more society-oriented than home-oriented. She's evolved a more vigorous physique, symbolic of her growing desire to get on in the world and achieve social and economic well-being.

II. Japanese Sex Practices

These conversations were held just before I left Japan, in the summer of 1969. I had been working closely on the translation and annotation of an ancient Chinese treatise on Taioist sexology with Dr Akira Ishihara,* a Japanese physician who was also a

*Dr Ishihara, born in 1924, widely travelled in Europe and Asia, with special emphasis on India, is a scholar of international repute. He speaks only Japanese but reads Chinese, English and German with facility, and likes to compose original Chinese verse. He has invaluable insights as to the nature of Asian medical practices and the inner structure of Asian societies.

medical historian and an expert in Chinese sexological traditions. We were chatting one evening in my home, when I suggested that we record our unrehearsed conversations for me to take back to the United States and translate, and Dr Ishihara enthusiastically agreed. At the time, we had been collaborating on 'The Tao of Sex' for about a year. We conversed in Japanese, and several months later I transcribed the two tapes and made the translations that follow.

I. FIRST CONVERSATION

L.: I have been living in Japan for eight years, but I know very little about Japanese sex practices. From what I've seen in Western writings, a couple of decades ago Japan for the foreigner was a place of free sex and uninhibited sexual behaviour. Many Westerners even today think of Japan and the Japanese in these terms; what is the truth?

I.: In ancient Japan, sex was regarded in a very free way. During the Tokugawa era (1603–1867), when feudalism flourished, many in the lower classes were economically harassed, and there were women who went into prostitution in order to ameliorate the poverty at home. The Yoshiwara brothels in Tokyo were one example of this practice.

L.: To many foreigners, free sex means a free association with women emancipated from the bonds of conventional morality. But, considering the Japanese propensity towards shyness and reserve, this question must be more complex than it appears at first glance.

I.: It is complex. Confucianism and Buddhism placed restrictions on the ruling classes, much like Catholicism in medieval Europe. But those who ruled the Japanese recognised that the masses had a right to enjoy sex, even though they were suppressed in other ways. A monogamous sytem of marriage was the principle from the beginning to the end of the era but, in spite of this, if a man liked another woman he was free to associate with her as he wished.

L.: But, for example, even in the Tokugawa era weren't women of the upper class confined all day as they were in China, concealed from male view? That being so, it was absolutely forbidden for them to associate with men until they married, wasn't it?

I.: You're right; the upper class treated their daughters as if they were kept in boxes. They couldn't walk outside the home alone,

16

and they couldn't fall in love and select a husband through personal choice. Proper Confucian upbringing decreed that they behave strictly in accord with the wishes of their parents.

L.: Was this limited only to a small number of the upper class, or was the concept also diffused among the masses?

I.: As education became widespread during the Tokugawa era, merchants and farmers outside the intellectual class acquired new learning and came to reject the idea that good lineage was all that mattered.

L.: Woman was relatively free in China until the tenth century; in the T'ang dynasty (618–906), for example, some of Emperor Hsüan-tsung's daughters married two and even three times. But, from about the mid-tenth century onwards, with the imposition of anti-female Confucian ideology, women became much more repressed and restricted. Did Japan develop in a similar way, with Confucianism forming a dividing line?

I.: Sex and divinity were considered one in Japan from earliest times, with sexual acts carried out in accord with the commands of the gods. Sex was a matter for holy reverence, and you didn't have sex with a partner you didn't prefer personally. In the Japan of pre-Nara times, say about fifteen hundred years ago, the doctrine that menstruation was unclean was not accepted. The association of menstruation and uncleanliness came into Japan with Buddhism. There is, for example, a love poem in the *Kojiki* (ca. eighth century *Chronicle of Ancient Events*) about a young man and woman. The woman goes to the man's house, and while she is there her skirt becomes soiled with blood. She not only does not become embarrassed, but she proudly shows this skirt to the man, who congratulates her for having entered into the cycle of menstruation that signifies womanhood. This is a matter for rejoicing; if they marry now, she can bear his children. Thus, menstruation was looked forward to in ancient Japan as a sign of healthy womanhood.

L.: That being so, was the onset of menstruation the occasion for a special congratulatory celebration?

I.: Yes, it was. This is no longer so, but until the start of the Meiji era (1868), in islands of the Izu Peninsula, the first menstruation was a time of rejoicing. There was a communal hut and, when the girl had her first menstruation, she left her home and went to the hut. When the sun came up on the following morning, all males who wanted to have sex with her could freely do so there. If she became pregnant as a result, she was considered to have consummated husband-wife relations. With the onset of the Meiji era, this type of behaviour was prohibited as being immoral, but I think it was an example of a very ancient Japanese custom being carried over until modern times.

L.: It may be of interest to note that this took place despite the emphasis of Shintosim, Japan's indigenous religion, on purity and on personal cleanliness.

I.: But menstruation was considered pure until the advent of Buddhism and its advocacy that menstruation was unclean. Prior to Buddhism sex, menstruation, and pregnancy were all regarded as the work of the gods. That's why you had to purify your person – what we call 'disinfecting'.

L.: Let's move on to the subject of virginity. When I spoke with the late Nagao Ryuzo (1884–1966) four or five years ago, he referred to a special Chinese custom that prevailed in Shantung Province earlier in this century. It seems that on the morning after the wedding night, the bride had to exhibit a blood-stained bed-sheet as proof of her having been a virgin bride. This would indicate that in the Chinese village premarital virginity was highly esteemed. Was there a similar outlook in Japan?

I.: Japan also regarded virginity as a serious matter, but with the view that one was defiled in giving up one's virginity unless the object was a true love union. It wasn't a case of losing or preserving virginity; when this happened through union with another sympathetic heart, the loss was considered a natural manifestation of the divine. This concept of morality changed with the intro-duction of Buddhism and Confucianism, and the rationale developed that children had to obey parental decrees and that girls must not lose their virginity without first securing the consent of the parents.

L.: When did this change take place?

I.: These concepts of morality did not prevail among the masses until the seventeenth century, when Confucian learning became widespread. Mass morality and upper-class morality differed.

L.: Then Japan was much later than China in the diffusion of Confucian thought.

I.: That's right.

L.: The following point is of special interest to me: When you compare the Manchu dynasty (1644–1910) in China with the Tokugawa era (1603–1867) in Japan, you'll note that while there was a prohibition against erotic writings in China, with relatively few being published, there was a profusion of erotic paintings and literary works in Japan. Could this have some bearing on the

18

differing pace of modernisation in the two civilisations? In other words, was there a correlation between the nature of sexual response and the attitude towards change?

I.: As I said before, Confucian thought in Japan did not prevail among the masses until a relatively late period. Prior to that time, sex in Japan was not considered 'free' but a manifestation entrusted to the gods. While Confucian-oriented intellectuals of the Tokugawa era tended to scorn erotic works, the masses were unaffected by this upper-class outlook. To them, eroticism was really something worth living for.

L.: In ancient China, on the wedding night, daughters of upper-class families might be shown erotic illustrations of intercourse. Was this type of sex instruction also practised in Japan?

I.: Yes, it was.

L.: When did this start?

I.: After the seventeenth century, when Confucian thought came to prevail. Sex education was provided for the daughter before she became a bride.

L.: Who furnished this instruction?

I.: In good families it was first given by the wet nurse, not by the mother.

L.: Did the wet nurse show the pictures?

I.: Yes, she did, explaining what the girl would have to do in order to have a baby. A characteristic of the Japanese bride was believed to be her ability to have a male child in the shortest time possible. She was to produce an heir and, in so doing, assure the continuity of the husband's line. Under the Confucian caste system enforced during the Tokugawa age, this was woman's destiny.

L.: Was the girl instructed when she became engaged, or was she taught the ways of love when she reached a certain age, say about fifteen?

I.: I think it was after the engagement and just before the marriage. For this purpose rich householders engaged artists to do the illustrations; these became the property of the bride.

L.: Did the groom explain or show these to her on the wedding night?

I.: I don't think they were shown then. Within the context of the Japanese class sytem, this kind of thing was considered rather burdensome. Marriages were arranged through a matchmaker, and if the bride failed to become pregnant after marriage, the matchmaker was deemed responsible. So he had to pay attention to the sex instruction aspect.

L.: The objective, then, was to bear children.

I.: That's right. In Tokugawa times, after the wedding the married couple didn't go off on a honeymoon like their Western counterparts.

L.: In China, on the wedding night, the guests might play various pranks in the bedroom; how about Japan?

I.: The Japanese didn't play such pranks; instead, the matchmaker stayed in a room next to that of the newlyweds until he was sure that the marriage act had been consummated.

L.: How could he do this, through the sounds that they made?

I.: He must have deduced it from what he heard. In extreme cases, not however, cited in documents, when the groom could not perform the marriage act the matchmaker entered the room and showed by example what had to be done.

L.: By that you mean. . . .

I.: The old matchmaker showed the groom how to have intercourse with the young bride. As he did this, with the ignorant young man by his side, the groom got excited and then had sexual relations with his bride. This signified that the matchmaker had fulfilled his responsibilities. This was one of the matchmaker's special rights, a most unusual one.

L.: Was this practised in the Tokugawa age?

I.: Yes, it was.

L.: Turning to a different subject, I've often heard it said that during the so-called Warring States period (1482–1558), Japanese warriors, in the absence of women, took along young boys and had sexual relations with them.

I.: This also occurred before the Warring States period; it was practised by monks.

L.: At about what time?

I.: From about the ninth century onwards. I think this custom first prevailed in India. You're probably aware that the Chinese character for haemorrhoids consists of elements meaning 'temple illness', an oblique reference to temple homosexuality. In other words, the anus was rent by the thrusts of the penis. This practice was alluded to in a Buddhist text in which the Buddha ostensibly explained how to cure 'temple illnesses'. There was concern with how to take care of bleeding from the anus that resulted from its being torn.

L.: There seem to be many Japanese illustrations of priests engaging in homosexuality.

I.: The most famous one is concealed in the Daigoji Temple at Kyoto as a secret treasure, not to be exhibited. The temple priests selected handsome young boy servants for this practice. The samurai took in boys from among the children of their sub-ordinates, and these boys served as personal secretaries and as homosexual partners.

L.: Did this custom become so well established that the average Japanese accepted it, something like the practice of homosexuality among the ancient Greeks?

I.: It was recognised, but under Confucianism the relationship was that of master and servant. The public role of the 'gay' youth was secretarial, the private role, homosexual.

L.: Homoxesuality in China seems to have flourished in the fifteenth and sixteenth centuries.

I.: In Japan, too, it was from the fifteenth to seventeenth centuries that homosexuality was most prevalent, a heritage of the Heian monks adopted by the samurai. The most famous practitioners were Oda Nobunaga and Toyotomo Hideyoshi. They both had young and handsome homosexuals at their sides.

L.: Did the wives of these samurai ever complain about this in verse or in prose?

I.: No, since that was an age in which such complaints could never be made. That's why the man could take concubines as he wished, without overt reaction from his wife. When the first wife failed to produce an heir, even in the case of an emperor a second, a third, and a fourth woman would be brought in until a male heir was produced; that child became the next emperor. The feudal lords naturally followed the emperor's example.

L.: To broach a different subject, in contemporary Japan one gets the impression that lesbianism is the most widespread homosexual relationship. Is this true?

I.: It is widespread, more so than male homosexuality, because of the way in which lesbianism flourished during the Tokugawa age.

L.: Why was that?

I.: The harem set-up among the upper class in Tokugawa Japan encouraged this; unlike China, eunuchs were never employed.*

L.: Here one can say, then, that Japan was impervious to Chinese influence.

I.: Eunuchs were used in China for two thousand years, from the Han dynasty (ca. 200 B.C.) onwards, but this practice never came into Japan.

L.: It can also be said that Japan was in no way influenced by the Chinese custom of foot binding.

*Chinese eunuchs could satisfy harem ladies through recourse to sexual means other than sexual intercourse, with some vestige of the man-woman relationship.

21

I.: That is correct. Getting back to the Japanese harem, there were only females in attendance there. A strict class system was observed among them; the *shogun* alone was free to do as he pleased in this woman's world. Male doctors did enter the harem on occasion, but there they were sometimes accused and heavily punished for committing even a slight breach in the prescribed social behaviour. This was an extremely strict system.

There were gradations among the concubines. The lowest-ranking women there, usually the youngest in the harem (between age fifteen and twenty), were required to simulate the role of the male. They had to satisfy the sexual needs of the high-ranking members of the harem. The harem girls in the lowest rank were called 'children of the rooms'.

L.: Were special implements used in the Japanese harem?

I.: Yes, various types – there was a special trade in these. The most popular implement in use was called a harigata; it was shaped like a penis and made from various materials. The most natural material was tortoise shell, which could be expanded and contracted.

L.: Didn't this injure the woman?

I.: I understand this was the most satisfactory material. It was not injurious; it became soft on being warmed, and therefore it had erotic implications.

L.: Is this still used in Japan?

I.: It's very expensive, so it can't be used very much. Plastic is probably considered the most satisfactory material now. In the days when tortoise shell was used, ivory was the next best material in quality.

L.: The use of ivory reminds one of the Chinese.

I.: Those who couldn't afford ivory used an implement made of wood. There were, of course, hard and soft wood, the hardest being the boxwood, which could expand and contract. A soft wood in use was the paulownia, but it would immediately become indented and therefore bruise.

There was a trader known as the *harigataya* who entered the inner quarters of the harem stealthily, bringing with him different sizes of *harigata* in a variety of materials.

L.: Two years ago, I met a lovely young geisha at a banquet who volunteered the comment that she was the female partner in a lesbian relationship. Is this common among the women who work the so-called 'water trade'* of Japan? Though these women in the bars and cabarets entertain an endless stream of male customers,

*Euphonious term for Japanese night life.

they cannot display too much affection towards one customer in particular, even if they want to. Do they therefore tend to reserve their deep and abiding affections for female co-workers? In other words, do they regard man-woman relations as a kind of business arrangement, devoid of deeper meaning? Looking at the matter psychologically, is this what one might expect?

I.: There are two aspects of the 'water trade', public and private. In the public aspect, since it's a business, no matter how many men the woman deals with, she lacks feelings towards them. But in the private aspect of sex, she either engages in lesbianism or uses masturbational implements.

L.: This must be a natural development, for in the course of business if she likes one customer too much it can result in financial loss. If he lacks money, or if another customer gets jealous as a consequence of her showing favouritism, she finds it difficult to earn the usual sums. In Japanese restaurants you sometimes see couples made up of a very feminine-looking female and a very masculine-looking one. The difference is startling; in these cases, would such women be from the 'water trade' or from the general class of society?

I.: Probably from the masses.

L.: Why is this so?

I.: When a normal male-female relationship is not realised – in other words, when the girl is unable to secure a fiancé – the alternative becomes lesbianism. The only other sexual outlet for her is masturbation.

L.: Japanese women may go to cocktail lounges in pairs or in groups, but they avoid going there alone. If they pair off with a male, it probably means that the couple is becoming serious. Is this an example of old traditional attitudes? Is it true that even today Japanese society looks askance on a man and woman walking together in public? If such is the case, then maybe it's natural for women to always be together. Therefore, there are many ways for a lesbian relationship to start.

I.: That is true; it probably indicates that even in our modern age some influences from Tokugawa-era Confucianism are still being felt. In other words, the belief exists that lesbians and male homosexuals do not lose their virtue, because the lovers are of the same sex. Confucius didn't say anything about this.

Perhaps this is even more so an aspect of Buddhism. In Hinduism, for example, where Hindu priests can't approach women or even talk to them, they naturally gravitate towards homosexuality in the temples. The Hindu nuns do likewise. This is probably a

23

natural religious misconception of what one should do in order not to break the taboo against male-female intercourse by priests and nuns.

L.: From my personal observation, it seems to me that girls from good Chinese and Korean families do not go out very much prior to marriage, even on group dates. The Japanese girl alone seems to be very active socially before marriage at the age of twenty-four or so.

I.: This has been true since the start of the Meiji era (1868). The Tokugawa age was extremely feudal, confined by Confucian-Buddhist concepts. But from mid-Meiji onwards – that is, from about the start of the twentieth century – European and American customs began to influence Japan. This was most noticeable among the upper classes, where free movement by girls of good families was regarded as a symbol of the new civilised behaviour.

L.: In this respect, Japan was again able to escape from the demand of Confucian ethics, distinguishing it from China and Korea. And, in a related sense, contemporary Chinese and Koreans place a high premium on the preservation of virginity by the bride. But in modern Japan, virginity isn't regarded as especially important, is it?

I.: No, it is still esteemed, and here is where we see a contradiction in the modernisation process in Japan. The ancient Buddhist-Confucian concepts permeate the Japanese person, who, however, appears on the surface to be completely emancipated and on the level of the civilisations of the West. These contradictions lodge in the one body side by side.

L.: I have been told there are Japanese women who, having lost their virginity, undergo an operation to restore a semblance of the hymen.

I.: This is propagandised in Japanese weekly journals, but it's a lie.

L.: This isn't being done?

I.: There are almost no cases of it.

L.: I thought the girl might do something like this before her wedding in order to deceive the groom.

I.: This time I'd like to ask *you* a question. The man who can tell on first intercourse if his partner is a virgin has to be a man of considerable experience, doesn't he? Too, girls who participate in sports like volleyball and ballet often tear the hymen in the process, even though they are virgins. Today's young Japanese girls are very active in sports and other activities, and, therefore, perhaps half of them have broken the hymen before the first intercourse. To rephrase this somewhat, the hymen that remains intact during vigorous and extended sports activities is not the kind that will be broken easily during the first intercourse.

L.: But is there some truth to the 'virginising' operation? Is the hymen-simulation claim, like the ads in Japanese journals about enlarging the penis, a medically valid one?

I.: The journals do publish these ads, but the claims that they make are extremely exaggerated. There may be some fraudulent quacks here and there who perform such operations.

L.: On a related subject, you said earlier that the matchmaker was responsible for all of the marital arrangements. Would he therefore make a verbal guarantee to the groom's parents to the effect that the prospective bride was a virgin?

I.: He generally bore that responsibility, though the matter was not discussed openly.

L.: But if she wasn't a virgin, what would the matchmaker's reaction be? One of anger?

I.: The matchmaker was highly respected, and his selection was considered to be morally appropriate. Following the wedding night, if the groom asserted that his bride was not a virgin her parents might counter by saying that only a man of wide experience could conclude this so quickly and that this cast doubt on the groom's moral character.

L.: This may be an exaggeration, but it seems to me that in the West individuals fall in love and marry without unduly considering the wishes of their parents or relatives. But in the East it used to be said that families, and not individuals, married. What are things like in modern Japan? Is the so-called arranged marriage really arranged?

I.: Today, the number of Japanese who marry entirely in conformity with the wishes of their parents, completely disregarding their own feelings, probably amounts to about 10 per cent of the total. These marriages prevail mostly in the villages. But now about 70 per cent of the marriages are probably made up of a 'half-and-half' composition of arranged-plus-love marriages. The other 20 per cent consist of love marriages entered into despite parental opposition.

L.: Are these on the increase?

I.: Yes, they are.

L.: When you say 'half and half', do you mean that the man and woman date first and then secure parental approval for getting married?

I.: Yes, I do.

L.: I may be entirely wrong, but in the West it appears that people

25

may fall passionately in love and marry, but when one day they undergo a change of heart many of them decide just as quickly on divorce. In Japan, it seems that men marry and start to produce children, and when they begin to lose interest at home they go out with male friends to various places of amusement. There are so many bars and cabarets in Japan that, while superficially enjoying a harmonious married life, men may conceal mistresses and in this way achieve a kind of balance between personal happiness and domestic obligation. But in America, there seems to be no way out other than the love marriage-loss or love-divorce syndrome.

I.: You're right, it seems to be 'yes or no' in the West. In Japan, there are, however, the ancient traditions transmitted through Buddhism and Confucianism, resulting in social restrictions on individual behaviour. The effort, then, becomes one of preserving harmony. To put it still more clearly, the inability to share this concept is one of the reasons why the percentage of failure in international marriages between Japanese and Americans is so high. The well-to-do merchants of the Tokugawa era usually had two or three concubines in addition to their wives, and there was a saying at the time to the effect that a man with only one wife was a failure (as a wage earner). This reminds one of the Islam religion, with its toleration of four wives. In Tokugawa Japan, the symbol of wealth was ownership of wife plus concubines.

L.: Is this concept still prevalent in Japan?

I.: Yes, among some old families – those which can trace their lineage at least as far back as the Tokugawa era.

L.: Is this an example of conspicuous affluence among the Japanese, an ostentatious display of wealth?

I.: The ostentatious display was in Tokugawa; today, because of the changes wrought by the Meiji era and our defeat in World War II, only a few families still maintain this way of thinking.

L.: In post war Japan, following the example of America, is there a clear tendency towards equality of the sexes? Is the status of women much improved over prewar times?

I.: Superficially, yes, but for the time being equality in the American sense cannot be achieved. This will probably take another fifty years.

L.: Why is this?

I.: It's because of our traditions, our Buddhist-Confucian traditions.

L.: Does the Japanese woman accept this as her fate, or is she demanding equality?

26

I.: There is considerable reaction among women over this, but their desire for equality has not yet made a social impact. That's why I say that in this regard Japan is fifty years behind America. Tokugawa feudalism lasted for three hundred years. It's true that in the hundred years since the inception of the Meiji era, European and American concepts of equality and democracy have exerted an influence on Japan, but this is a problem involving changes in deep-rooted ways of thinking. To me, it's comparable to the centuries after Martin Luther appeared that it took for Protestantism to establish its own world. In the case of Japan, it will not take three centuries, but it will certainly take a century and a half (starting with the Meiji era) to achieve the sexual equality of European-American societies.

II. SECOND CONVERSATION

L.: In 1947, when I thought of applying to enter graduate school at Harvard, I had a conversation in Cambridge with Professor Eliseef, and I remember how he contrasted Western sex practices with those of the Japanese. He said that Westerners resorted to the kiss as a prelude to intercourse but that with the Japanese the kiss followed intercourse.
I.: There are references to the kiss and to foreplay in Tokugawa texts. In the early nineteenth century, there was a very popular design in the form of lips on cotton kimono. Kimono so designed were then considered the height of fashion, but after fifteen years they were officially prohibited. The kiss did not become generally popular until the Meiji era, but the union of two pairs of lips was an inevitable development.
L.: Did the Japanese emulate the so-called French kiss, touching tongue to tongue?
I.: The kiss was called *sashimi* (raw slices of fish) in Japanese, with the tongue not penetrating the other's mouth. Only the lips touched; hence the analogy to the look of *sashimi*. Because the tongue did not penetrate, sexual excitement was probably further heightened.
L.: Is the kiss now a prelude to intercourse, as in the West?
I.: Yes, it is, but there are different stages of progression. These can be discussed later.
L.: Western lovers say things like 'I love you', but this expression seems to defy literal translation into Japanese. Do the Japanese use a similar expression? If so, what is its history?

27

I.: Poetry was the medium for expressing love, both in the Heian and later eras. The Yoshiwara was a representative quarter of prostitution in Tokugawa Japan, where prostitutes might write poems to customers with whom they fell in love. While one could not say things like 'Please come again' in Japan in a love situation, a sentiment like this would be expressed in a poem.

L.: How long did this custom continue?

I.: Until about the end of the nineteenth century; ancient eighth-century poetic forms were used.

L.: What about the present-day Japanese?

I.: They lack the kind of learning needed to compose poetry.

L.: That being so, do they borrow Western expressions like 'I love you'?

I.: Yes, they do.

L.: What about the term *horeta*?

I.: This is equivalent to the Western term 'love' in the sense of being enraptured by someone and by only that person. But because of remaining Confucian influence, the Japanese avoid expressing their feelings in a frank and open way.

L.: In America, on the verge of emission one may use the term 'coming', but in Korea the word used means 'doing', while in Japan one speaks of 'going'. Is there some psychological basis for this distinction between 'coming' and 'going'?

I.: Not to change the subject, the word for this differs even in Japan itself in the Kanto and Kansai areas. In Kanto one ordinarily uses 'going', but in Kansai one says instead that 'it's already finished'.

L.: In Korea, sexual references to death are often heard, concerning the non-erect state of the penis, for example. What about in Japan?

I.: The Japanese often say 'Dying, dying, dying', but this is most common in the Kansai region.

L.: Under what circumstances, and by whom?

I.: At the time of climax, by the woman. Prior to that one says 'Going, going, going' – the process is from 'going' to 'dying'.

L.: On another subject, I was startled to hear that Japanese men still strike women in anger. This is common in Korea, but how about Japan? This is probably relatively rare in the West.

I.: I think it's the same in the West, as one aspect of sadism and masochism. It's the same everywhere.

L.: Do you mean the striking is done, not in anger, but for sexual reasons?

I.: Don't misunderstand me, but in a platonic sense I am familiar

28

with women from South-east Asia to Europe, and it seems to me that Caucasians show a definite preference for masochism.

L.: Is the man the one who prefers it, with the woman beating him? Does the male then incline towards femininity?

I.: Yes, that's right.

L.: Is the sex life of the Japanese gradually changing due to post-war influences?

I.: Since the war, Japan has been gravitating towards a Western style of behaviour.

L.: This so-called Western style includes the elevation of women; in the days of the troubadours, she was placed on a pedestal and worshipped. But exalting women in this way never was done in the East, was it?

I.: You're right, it never was.

L.: In looking at Japan for the past twenty-five years, what changes in sexual attitudes have occurred and what changes do you see in the future?

I.: There is a sharp division in Japan, evolving from the destruction of the traditional feudal, Confucian-oriented family system. This is postwar Japan's most significant movement. However, such things as a form of arranged marriage will probably remain to some extent for at least another thirty years.

L.: There are many articles in Western magazines about how women insist that the male satisfy their sexual desires. These women complain, for example, when the male has an orgasm before they have had one.

I.: May I question you on this point?

L.: Please go right ahead.

I.: Caucasian peoples probably grant the woman a divorce in the event that the male is unable to fulfill his proper role, but in Japan, with its history of fifteen hundred years of Confucianism, feudal ways of thought have not yet disappeared. For example, there was a statement in the news recently by a famous young Japanese radical labour leader to the effect that he would select a bride only in accordance with the wishes of his parents.

L.: Won't Japanese women follow the Western pattern and begin to make demands of their mates?

I.: There is some talk about this of late, but among older families it is still inconceivable.

L.: Millions of American women now take 'the pill' as a contraceptive, what about the Japanese?

I.: They don't use it at all.

L.: Is it because they feel it's dangerous?

I.: I'll change the subject slightly. There are still two thousand villages in Japan without doctors, and many of our so-called 'doctors' are not really qualified.

L.: Do the males usually use contraceptives?

I.: Yes, on the intellectual level, but in the villages there is little or no economic surplus.

L.: When they don't want children, then, do they have abortions?

I.: That's the point. In the Tokugawa era, from the seventeenth to the end of the nineteenth centuries, medicine did not progress and there were few doctors. In such circumstances, infanticide was practised. It was an era when Buddhism was weak, Christianity was forbidden, and Shintoism lacked the power to lead.

L.: Will Japanese women also start to use the pill?

I.: This question will be tied to economics. For example, even condoms are expensive – the cheapest are twenty-five cents a dozen, the best, a dollar a dozen.

L.: Why won't the Japanese in the future do research on the pill, the way they did with cameras, in order to come up with an inexpensive product for world-wide export?

I.: There would be the problem of the market for it.

L.: There's a tremendous market for the pill in the United States because it's a very convenient device.

I.: But as I, a Japanese physician, see it, one still can't be sure about it. This will become a more serious problem in the future.

L.: Because of the individual differences among women who use it?

I.: Yes, that's right.

L.: On this point, then, the United States and Japan differ completely.

In our country, engaged couples have considerable freedom in their sexual relations. What about the Japanese? Does engagement usually precede marriage?

I.: About one-third get engaged. As late as the nineteenth century there was a Japanese custom called 'entering the feet' (ashi-ire). A man who loved a woman might enter her home for one or two years, regardless of parental opposition.

L.: Was there a contract?

I.: No, this practice wasn't sanctioned legally. The man might simply say, 'Today I'm tired, so I'll stay (the night).'

L.: Didn't the parents oppose this?

I.: No, since it meant part-time help for them. The parents then decided if this was a true match, depending on such things as whether or not the couple had sexual relations.

L.: Divorce in the West is often difficult to secure; one needs to hire a lawyer, have a valid excuse, etc. Divorce is complex and time consuming.

I.: In Japan, there was no concept of a lawyer until the Meiji era, for in feudal times judgements were rendered by the feudal lords. And no one could complain. The lord, with the power of a god, could order the parties to wed, and his will had to be obeyed. Love was beside the point.

L.: What are things like today?

I.: Divorce in Japan is now western style; but as late as the Tokugawa era there were no lawyers, and the judge decided everything.

L.: Were divorces simply arranged?

I.: On the contrary, they were even more complex than the Chinese divorce of Ming-Ch'ing times.

L.: I read an interesting article about remarriage in one of the Japanese mass-circulation magazines, in which the point was made that divorced Japanese women seldom re-wed. This differs sharply from the West, where divorcees often marry a second time. Is the problem in Japan one of shame or of feudal thinking?

I.: It's of feudal thinking, not shame, with both families involved. The concept is Confucian, without primary concern for husband and wife. The meaning of family in Japan is much broader than the American idea of 'my home'.

L.: The family is often just the two parties in the West.

I.: That's right. But in Japan, for example, taking care of the parents is one of your first duties. And then there are other dependents.

L.: I'm embarrassed to mention this, but I once saw an ad in the *Japan Times* about an operation for enlarging the penis. Is this common?

I.: No, although it exists. It is probably resorted to much more by foreigners who visit this country than by the Japanese. The belief that the large penis is stronger and the smaller one weaker is erroneous.

L.: In the Chinese novel *Prayer Mat of Flesh* (*jou-p'u t'uan*), certain statements imply that traditional Chinese thinking equated the size of the penis with efficaciousness – the larger the better. Little attention was paid to stimulation of the woman's erogenous areas, and the emphasis was on depth of penetration. The late R. H. van Gulik's extensive research on Chinese sex practices seems to substantiate this. Perhaps the Japanese were so influenced by this theory of the Chinese that they, also, became

31

absorbed in the problem of size.

I.: To tell the truth, the Japanese don't enjoy foreplay and they don't like to delay the climax.

L.: Then they must be rather quick about the sex act.

I.: Yes, perhaps quicker than in the West. Japanese women have asserted that foreigners take too long to reach a climax because they are incapable of doing otherwise. Eastern men differ sharply in their approach to this.

L.: In the West, the man often awaits the woman's climax before he emits. Is this also true in Japan?

I.: The Japanese male also emits after his partner's climax.

L.: Do the Japanese perform the sex act a second and third time?

I.: To be considered capable in sex, the male must be able to repeat the act.

L.: What about fellatio and cunnilingus? Are these practised much less in Japan than in the West?

I.: Western women may engage in fellatio, but this is virtually unknown in Japan.

L.: Do the males practise cunnilingus of the female?

I.: They do not.

L.: There must be major differences, then, between East and West in sexual techniques and practices?

I.: One reason for this is that the construction of the Japanese home is paper-thin.

L.: Can these acts be easily seen?

I.: No, but the slightest sounds can be heard.

L.: That being so, do women avoid making any sound?

I.: Yes, that's where the problem is; but now more and more apartments are being built.

L.: Regarding free sex, it seems to me that even within a so-called free context the Japanese woman remains shy and prefers sex under the covers. She avoids being seen in the nude, even by her bed partner. Perhaps this, too, is an aspect of Confucianism.

I.: In general, sex in Japan doesn't take place either totally in the nude or with the lights on.

L.: As western-style houses are built, will this behaviour change?

I.: Yes, but it will take about thirty years.

L.: I read an article in a Japanese journal alleging that the Western penis was larger but the Japanese penis harder.

I.: That's true, the Eastern penis is harder.

L.: What's the scientific reason for this?

I.: The difference between a meat diet and the vegetarian diet generally followed throughout the East, including India.

32

L.: Because erotic Japanese prints formerly depicted grotesquely large penises, the Japanese acquired a reputation in Europe for unusual size.

I.: And now they're said to be small. That's not so; the truth is completely different.

L.: Perhaps Westerners are unaware of this factor of hardness

I.: That's probably true.

L.: What positions of intercourse do the Japanese prefer?

I.: The most popular is the one with the man above the woman, but there's been a recent change towards the woman's being positioned above the man. This is a definite change for Japan. It isn't assumed right away – at first, the man is on top, but the woman gets on top after she's become excited. One-third of Japanese sexual relations are probably like this.

L.: How many positions do the Japanese try prior to climax?

I.: Generally three.

L.: What's the third one?

I.: Recently the trend is for the woman to coil the left leg and place the right leg below the man's head. They then move back and forth.

L.: This is alluded to in the old Chinese novels, but it must have been much more popular in the East than the West.

Eleven years ago, prostitution in Japan was legally forbidden. That being so, how do the present-day youth get their sexual experience?

I.: They probably don't go all the way, stopping with petting. They meet, are attracted to one another, and then pet. Kissing follows the petting.

L.: Are you saying that young Japanese males are still virgins before marriage?

I.: Yes, I am. There's a current idea in Japan that one marries *because* one has become intimate with a member of the opposite sex. This is the exact opposite of the way things used to be.

L.: Before the war, when prostitution flourished, would the father take the son to famous quarters like the Yoshiwara for his initiation into sex? This was sometimes done in the West.

I.: The situation varied according to the father's occupation and the historical epoch.

L.: On another subject, recently, in a popular Western journal, the writer alleged that married Japanese take mistresses.

I.: That was true for the Tokugawa era, but not for today.

L.: What about the geisha? Does she still have a patron, as in former times?

I.: This can be thought of, in European terms, as having one's private secretary.

L.: Does 'private' here mean being a secretary and nothing more?

I.: The relationship may go further, but not necessarily.

L.: But she's a lot more expensive than other secretaries, isn't she?

I.: Not at all.

L.: Oh, I thought there was a cost of several million yen involved. Doesn't the patron buy her clothes and such?

I.: He may buy her clothes, but that's a different question. Caucasians often come to Japan with the warped opinion that if a woman is yellow skinned, anything goes. But it's not that simple. A man may tell a geisha, 'I've become enthralled by your talents; please serve as my secretary.' That's all there may be to it.

Dewi in Indonesia* is a typical case, and there are many Japanese women like her in Hong Kong and other nearby countries. To put it succinctly, aside from the matter of morals it's probably natural for the woman to give service to the patron who has become enraptured by her sexuality. This is true regardless of race.

L.: Will the present geisha system continue? The woman who works in a cabaret can earn her money directly and without the involved feudal relationships that surround the geisha.

I.: The geisha system will probably disappear within thirty years.

L.: The *kiseng* in Korea serve the man in every respect; maybe the geisha were that way, too, before the war. The *kiseng* concentrates on pleasing the customer, without the aloofness of the geisha.

I.: Japan is now one of the advanced nations of the world, not a backward one. The *kiseng* have their counterparts throughout Asia, in Hong Kong, Taipei, Bangkok, and Singapore.

L.: Did you see the article in a Chinese newspaper this spring about a Japanese in Taipei who was arrested for being with a prostitute? Was this news item picked up in Japan? The Chinese must have gotten very angry to sacrifice him like that.†

I.: I really don't know what the story was.

L.: Frank Harris and other Western writers earlier in this century often claimed the Japanese were uninhibited sexually. But the question really isn't that simple, is it?

I.: Japan was backward forty or fifty years ago; the people were penniless. As long as the Caucasians paid in dollars, they could do whatever they wanted.

* The late Sukarno's Japanese wife, a former bar hostess.
† Prostitution is widespread in Taiwan.

34

L.: So the primary reason was economic.

I.: The old guidebooks implied that the geisha was at the customer's beck and call. The Caucasians responded to the implication but were disappointed. Japan may have once been Mount Fuji, cherry blossoms, and geisha, but that's no longer true. Until 1920, foreigners were drawn to Japan solely by these attractions. The young geisha of today, the so-called *maiko* still in training, are all busy mastering English. There's a special school for them; when this happens, it means their customers must be other than Japanese.

L.: Then they probably have a tie-in with tourist agencies.

I.: It's the same with the *kiseng* in Seoul.

L.: But it's rare to find a *kiseng* who speaks Japanese or English, isn't it? They're young, in their early twenties.

I.: The *maiko* of the Gion quarter in Kyoto has to learn English by the age of twenty to be considered qualified. That's why, unfortunately, profligate foreigners often come to these quarters.

L.: I'd like to change to still another subject. You said earlier that the ancient Japanese rejoiced at the onset of menstruation. How did the present attitude come about?

I.: Buddhism proclaimed that woman was defiled by sin and evil by nature.

L.: Who explains the meaning of menstruation to the daughter — the mother?

I.: It's done in the school, where sex education is introduced by the third year of elementary school. At the age of nine, boys and girls are given explanations of sex in separate classes.

L.: Doesn't this have a revolutionary significance for the Confucian-oriented Japanese family?

I.: It's definitely a revolution, a great revolution.

L.: Is the school starting to replace the home?

I.: Yes, that's why Japan is in for trouble. It needs qualified teachers, but its present teachers, for the most part, are little more than skilled workers.

L.: Then will the schools form a bridge between East and West, transforming Japan from Confucianism to Western orientation?

I.: Sex education, if conducted in an open and scholarly way, should become a positive factor in social enlightenment. The Japanese are still hampered by Confucianism, but not to the extent that the Chinese and Koreans are. The rest of the East will be influenced by Confucianism for another fifty years, twenty years behind Japan. In other words, it will take another fifty years

35

III. Free Marriage, Free Love

Free marriage and free love probably flourished in ancient Japan, since there are no early records of arranged marriages and politically-contrived marriages. According to ancient myths, women might first make love with a man and then ask for their parents' permission to marry, which indicates that love, and not virginity, was the prerequisite to matrimony. The ancient rulers had many concubines, however, and they had a high regard for female chastity; while they maintained a double standard and had many women, their women were expected to remain true to one man.

In the age of mythology, men and women fought alongside one another. But only women were allowed to serve the gods because their ability to conceive was associated with fertility beliefs.

The *Kojiki* ('Chronicle of Ancient Events', early eighth century) implies that, unless she was in love, even a poor working girl might reject an emperor.

There were no beds or mattresses in ancient days; couples made love in the grass, in the woods, or in huts in the fields. Men and women wore simple one-piece garments, so simple that when they wished they could unfasten one string and immediately become nude. There was no paper available, so after intercourse they probably wiped themselves with grass or did not cleanse at all.

IV. Group Courtship, Betrothal

There was a custom of group marriage in ancient Japan involving young men and women who assembled in the mountains or in certain other designated areas in spring and autumn. They would eat and drink, dance and sing, and through their songs the men would seek wives. This custom seems to have continued until about the start of the eighth century. Rivals for a woman competed for her through poetic competition; a man and woman might sing of their feelings and then fall in love. Legend has it that one such couple spent the night together right on the spot where they had fallen in love and were so embarrassed at being discovered by the local villagers that they transformed themselves into pine trees. In one instance the men sang from one mountain peak while the women sang from a peak adjacent to it. Twice yearly, as spring and autumn arrived, men and women of appropriate age brought food, wine, and lutes and assembled at predetermined places. There they engaged joyfully in choral contests, obeying the rule that unless he won out in competition the man could not make the woman his own. There is a poem extant about the man who was rejected by a lover who failed to keep their rendezvous. Another male poet confessed that, having lost out in competition, he had to sleep alone. Women were ashamed to return home from these assemblages without having been at least 'wives for a night'. It was more a marriage by choice than by random coupling, although at these gatherings sexual relations were freely permitted.

The victorious male could do with his mate as he pleased. The woman also had to master songs, for if she lost she had to accept the male, attracted to him or not. The competitors learned certain words and certain poetic forms, with the *tanka* (five, seven, five, seven, seven syllables) poetic form favoured.

Later, the nature of the song contest changed, with not only unmarried males but men with wives participating as well. Thus the choral contest evolved into a festival of profligation. One song in the *Manyoshu* (sixth-to-eighth-century collection of poetry) alludes to participation in these contests by married men and women: 'On that day, it was all right for another man to take my wife. The god of the mountain from times long past has allowed this, so whatever one did on that day was permissible.'

The origin of this custom of free sexual relations in Japan is unknown. The festival at first was a place for selecting a wife; later, it became an occasion for the free and indiscriminate choosing of a mate. On this day wives and husbands were free to enjoy sex with others. Perhaps married women joined in the festivities because their husbands had failed to provide them with children and they sought fertility through other men. Or perhaps husbands and wives attended because as time went on the rules were relaxed. In antiquity, pregnancy was a divine mystery and the

37

Japanese may not have been cognisant of who impregnated the female. To them, the woman who conceived during a holy festival did so through the help of the gods.

TRIAL MARRIAGE IN EARLY JAPAN

Premarital experimentation in ancient Japan was not considered lewd, but rather a proper preparation for marriage. The custom was called *yobai*. In other words, the man went to the home of the woman with the intention of marrying her. This was sung about in the *Manyoshu* to the effect that a poet found the right woman in a nearby region only to be with her too short a time – before he knew it dawn had arrived. With the first crow of the cock, the man had to leave his lover's arms and head for home.

There were no arranged marriages of convenience as yet during this age; after they had reached an agreement, the man usually went to visit his intended's home. An engagement of sorts was entered into but no rings were exchanged and their relatives were not apprised. The lovers discussed their plans, the man sleeping with the woman night after night. Society recognised them as husband and wife only after they had a child. Or the man and woman could become husband and wife by setting up their home independently. If they became alienated, the union was simply dissolved.

OTHER ASPECTS OF TRIAL MARRIAGE

The so-called *ashi-ire* ('putting one's feet in') trial marriage resembled the *yobai*, except that in this case the woman usually went to the man's house. In one village in Kyushu, for example, the woman moved to the man's home in a spirit of trial marriage but with a very casual attitude. Socially speaking, she was not considered married and she was not referred to publicly as a bride. If she did not get along well with the man's parents, she could be sent back to her own home. In that Kyushu village there was no demand that the bride be a virgin, so no matter how many men she slept with on a trial basis her reputation was unimpaired. One important factor in the success or failure of this arrangement was her ability to work in the fields and fulfill all domestic tasks required of her by her prospective in-laws.

V. Communally Possessed Maidenheads

In Japan, the right to deflower a virgin was not necessarily the prerogative of the groom. In one remote area called Shiriyami-saki,* for example, until about the start of the Meiji era (1868) village girls and divorced women had to serve as communal property of the village youths. When girls reached fifteen, they were placed in a special house where they had to obey any and all demands made of them by young males. If they obstinately resisted such demands they were severely disciplined. The youth thus rebuffed by one of the girls reported the incident to her parents and at the same time spread this fact throughout the village. The girl's father and elder brothers had the duty to convince the recalcitrant girl of the rashness of her ways. They might shut her up in a single room for as long as two weeks in order to bend her will to conform with village mores, and if she continued to resist because of what was criticised by the community as egoistic stubbornness, she then faced expulsion from the village. In contrast to this collective sexual obligation, the girls were forbidden to have anything to do with outsiders. If they did, they could similarly be banished. The sanction of sexual license in Shiriyam-isaki must have been the vestige of a very old custom whereby the girls of the village were regarded as communal property of the young men.

There were similar customs practised in other parts of Japan. In Echigo County, for example, wives were drawn by lot on the Festival of All Souls Day, which fell on the fifteenth day of the seventh lunar month. On this day young men of the villages would choose wives from among the village girls by drawing lots for them. A girl chosen by lot had to suppress any adverse feelings and blindly obey the man who had won her. But if the male did not like her, he could release her through the simple purchase of a few quarts of wine. At the time of the yearly drawing, the youths would be in high spirits as they summoned the girls. In Echigo County, therefore, it was believed that the God of Love

*Wakamori Taro and others, *Gisei no hitobito* (Sacrificed People). Tokyo, Mainichi shimbusha, 1969, pp. 24–30. I have made extensive use of this book for the 'Right of the first night' and other related information that it contains. Cf. the extensive monograph by Nakayama Taro, *Nihon koninshi* (A History of Marriage in Japan) Tokyo, Shunyodo, 1928, 8–60; it is fully annotated.

39

favoured the random selection of a wife. When the number of single men and women failed to balance, blank lots were included in the drawing in appropriate numbers, and those who drew such lots had to retreat to the side-lines until the following year. The lottery would seem to indicate that there, as well, the girls were considered communal property, the ownership of whom was left to chance.

In Iwasa County, Fukushima Prefecture, when a girl came of age the village youths would meet and delegate one of their number to advise the girl's family that she was not yet a woman and would therefore have to be made into one. It was the custom there to summon her and to 'make her into a woman' on the fifteenth night of the first lunar month. There are records that this also occurred in Ashikaga District in 1892 and 1893. In Togo County, Iwate Prefecture, on All Souls Day the village lads and lasses engaged in a rope-pulling contest which each side strove to win. That night, fourteen girls had to offer their maidenheads to the youths. This practice persisted into the Meiji era, for as late as 1887 a critic of Japanese morals called in print for its abolition, describing it as dissolute.* The Ministry of the Interior supported youth organisations adamantly opposed to the coercive sexual habits of such village youths, and they made a determined effort to eliminate what were regarded officially as squalid customs.† With the Meiji era, the rights of the father came to supercede those hitherto enjoyed by the village youths.

VI. Premarital Sex (*Yobai*)

There are still remnants of the practice of *yobai* in contemporary Japanese farm villages, but in tracing its historical origins the cruelty exercised against women again comes to the fore. The term *yobai* may have been originally derived from the word *yobo*, meaining 'to try to call out to someone'. It would therefore refer to trying to communicate one's emotions and, by extended connotation, to seeking marriage. The term also was taken to mean 'visiting a woman under the cover of night'. Until the Heian era

*Ibid., p. 26, q.v.
†Ibid., loc. cit.

(ninth century), marriage took place through the man's going to the woman's home to seek a wife, with *yobai* generally used in later epochs to designate the unmarried male who went to a woman's home for sexual purposes.

The custom of *yobai* continued to be observed for a long time in Japanese villages throughout the land, but it would be misleading to interpret its existence as a sign of the emancipation of women. It took place in a feudal society dominated by a patrilineal family system, and it was common for the girl's feelings to be ignored and for the issue to be decided according to the man's wishes alone. There were even instances in which the practice of *yobai* was tantamount to rape and to public acceptance of the rape. Since there was a popular saying in the villages to the effect that a girl who had not been subjected to *yobai* would never get a mate, the parents pretended not to be aware of its less savoury aspects.

But in districts where the girl's feelings were taken into account, it did become to some extent an exercise in free love. In Kagoshima's Ibusuki County, for example, when the girl came of age her parents had her sleep between them. If there was a boy whom she liked, the girl accepted him into the bed. But if she was averse to accepting him, she would tap her mother with her foot, her mother would inform the father, and the boy would be driven from the house. This variation of *yobai* is said to have been practised all over Japan.* In north-eastern districts, kindling might be placed at the entrance to the girl's house so that, if she wished to repulse the male invader, she could ask her father to beat the youth with the sticks of wood close at hand.

There were regulations and taboos in regard to *yobai*, enforced by special organisations of village youths who taught and preserved the 'unwritten laws' that had to be obeyed. In certain districts in Kochi Prefecture, for example, the male had to approach the girl he wanted through a go-between in the village organisation. The go-between had the right of defloration, after which the young man was allowed to approach the girl. If the girl was violated by an outsider, youths from the village organisation would join together to thrash the transgressor. She and the outsider might be stripped nude, bound, and dragged around the village.

In every area there was also a feminine counterpart of the young men's organisation. In Tottori and Kochi Prefectures, for

*Inoue Kazuo, *Zankoku no Nihonshi* ('A History of Cruel Japan'), Tokyo, Kappa Books, 1969, p. 208.

41

example, when the girl turned thirteen the rights of ownership over her were said to be transferred from her parents to the village. The thirteen-year-old girls lived together in a fixed place, forming a sort of YWSO (Young Women's Sex Organisation), where they received sex instruction from their elders. The YMSO (Young Men's Sex Organisation) and the YWSO might meet together nightly, with the girls listening to male talk about sex. But in general there were far fewer YWSO than YMSO. There were also reports of organisations through which men and women slept together and had random sexual relations. In southern Ehime Prefecture, until the Taisho era (1912–25), there were twenty-one such communal sex organisations. In 1850, in a village called Taromaru, there is a record of fourteen- and fifteen-year-old girls who entered the local YMSO, where they were treated like women. They were also used in sexual transactions involving visitors to the region.

The practice of *yobai* might be interpreted as a stepping stone towards a free choice in marriage. In farming and fishing villages around the Inland Sea, girls and boys who had had sexual relations called one another by special names and could marry if they chose, despite parental opposition. If a publicly recognised *yobai*-type union was later rejected by the girl, she was ostracised by the villagers.

SIMULATED MARRIAGE ABDUCTIONS

One cannot, however, without qualification equate *yobai* with a marriage based on freedom of choice. The girl had little choice and the man could persist even if she rejected him. And if she repeatedly refused him, she was scorned by the village. In extreme cases, she might even be derided as a freak of nature (*katawamono*). There were many instances in which the girl surrendered her flesh because she feared censure from the village if she acted otherwise. By the Yedo era (early seventeenth century), the male also could not ordinarily make a choice that went against the wishes of the girl's father, whose consent to the marriage was considered mandatory. Legally, free marriage was denied – there had to be parental permission. Following Chinese Confucian dicta, boys and girls in feudal Japan were kept apart from the age of seven on, so *yobai* constituted the only way through which men and women could traverse the barriers imposed by a closed society. For poor men and women in farming and fishing villages, and especially for the men, *yobai* symbolised rare and mysterious pleasures.

One variation of the practice was called *yome-katsugi* (literally, 'carrying a bride on one's back'). This widespread custom was both a reaction against a closed society and a remnant of more primitive times. The form it took in Japan was for the village association of youths to carry a girl off on their backs and to coerce her into marrying the young man who was trying to win her. This was done all over Japan, referred to by names which differed from one locality to the next.

In the Aki region of Tosa, the male who wanted to marry a certain girl applied to do this through the YMSO. If the YMSO agreed, he and five or ten other young men went to the girl's house. They chose a time when she usually left the house and then abducted her by force. If the abduction succeeded, they had one of their group guard her while the others shouted to the parents inside her house that so-and-so had abducted her. A betrothal present was then usually presented through the auspices of a YMSO representative. The village leader was visited next and asked to assent to the marriage. The YMSO usually got its way, but sometimes upper-class families who revered their lineage would try to recover the abducted daughter. This type of marriage abduction, although under frequent official prohibition, continued in the Tosa district until after 1868 and the start of the Meiji era. And even after that, abduction might be encouraged by parents who wanted to eliminate the expenses of a wedding celebration. This is reminiscent of the Ainu custom of carrying off the girl on a specified night in order to avoid the cost of a formal wedding.

There were abductions, then, in Japan in which the girl's feelings were totally ignored. Sometimes real force was used, and the marriage became one founded on rape or coercion. Despite the use of force, if the matchmaker intervened and the girl's parents consented, a marriage could be transacted. But in other instances the girl was well acquainted with the youth and received him cheerfully. She could indicate she accepted him by partaking of the food which the groom-to-be offered her. She might also blacken her teeth, symbolic of the married woman. If the girl seemed unwilling, the young man might try to blow the teeth-blackening ingredients into her mouth to make it appear that she accepted him.

VII. The Right of the First Night

In ancient China, the loss of a girl's virginity was referred to as 'breaking the melon'. The Japanese adopted this expression, adding the interpretation that since the Chinese character for 'melon' might be analysed as consisting of two 'eights', it meant that the girl 'broke her melon' at the age of sixteen. With the rupture of the hymen, the blood that was spilled was regarded with awe and fear, something to be shunned. That is why, in order to alleviate the fear of the pain and the bleeding and to afford protection to the young couple from harm by evil spirits, there were priests, doctors, shamans, and other holy men who sacrificed themselves for the cause and had intercourse with the virgin in place of the groom. This has been referred to as the *droit du signeur*, or 'the right of the first night'. Similar customs were observed in medieval Europe and practised widely in India and Africa as well as Japan. However, not only Japanese holy men but rulers, landowners, landlords, and go-betweens also took it upon themselves to perform this function as a kind of public duty or as one of the privileges of rank. If a ruler exercised the privilege, any heir conceived about the time of the first-night encounter was regarded as possibly the ruler's child and accorded free status as a consequence.

Certain tribes living among the Chinese, like the Tibetans and the Turks in the north-west, were disinclined to marry virgins.* They would first present them to a Buddhist priest to be deflowered, after which they were considered eligible for marriage. The masses believed that in adhering to this custom they were affording pleasure to their gods. There was also the practice of having a go-between deflower the maiden before she was given away in marriage – he was thereby able to vouch for her virginity. One method of defloration in common use among Chinese Mohammedans and performed on ten year-old girls (with sadistic intent?) was referred to as 'opening the closed'. Such girls usually couldn't stand up for several days afterwards and, in extreme cases, they became disabled. The scholar who has profound

*The information about these tribes in China is based on the monograph by Hirosato Iwai called, 'The Buddhist Priest and the Ceremony of Attaining Womanhood during the Yüan Dynasty', Toyobunko (Memoirs), No. 7, 1935, 105–161.

knowledge of this subject, Professor Iwai, declines to associate it with 'right of the first night' privileges and instead interprets it as a sacred religious duty, performed by priests revered by the masses. A Chinese reference to the way Cambodians deflorated virgins towards the turn of the thirteenth century states that 'when the moment arrives the priest enters the room with the damsel and, taking away her virginity with one of his fingers, puts it into wine'. Viewed in religious perspective, therefore, defloration through resort to intercourse instead of the priestly fingers may have represented a deviation from the holy solemnity of the original observance. Professor Iwai concludes that solemnity and care characterised the priestly defloration ceremony, with no lascivious or obscene implications.*

In Japan, there were cases in which a father with children might rupture hymens as a regular business, though without having sex with the bride. He might, for example, be paid for using his fingers to 'break the melon'. To avoid having to accept a bureaucrat endowed with first-night privileges, certain districts in Japan paid a so-called virgin tax. Our Japanese researcher states there were old men in the Ikegawa region of Kochi Prefecture who conducted 'the right of the first night' until extremely recent times. He goes on to list five other prefectures in which either elders or go-betweens did the 'melon-breaking', although in the Ryukyus and in Awagishima it was done by youths.

In the flower-and-willow world of organised prostitution, there was a practice called *mizu-age* in which a wealthy man or a prospective patron purchased the right to break the hymen of the geisha-to-be for a goodly sum. These sales seem to be transacted secretly even to the present day. The term *mizu-age*, which literally means 'to raise out of the water', as in catching a fish, apparently originated as a literary metaphor for defloration. Therefore, it could also be interpreted as 'to hook a virgin'.

There was a very ancient belief in Japan that a virgin should offer herself up to the gods. Then there evolved the concept that the next-best offering was to the man who represented the gods – in other words, the man in charge of the shrine. Other men of distinction in certain localities likewise came to possess 'the right of the first night'.

The idea that the virgin was to be enjoyed collectively by the youths of her village must have been allied to the idea that her virginity was not an exclusive possession of the groom. During

*Ibid., op. cit., 152–3. Iwai (p. 157) further notes that, according to the Veda, blood flowing from the first intercourse had in it a venomous poison, the root of all evils.

the Yedo era (1603–1867), here and there throughout Japan it was habitual for someone other than the groom to be entrusted with deflowering the bride. In some places, the groom could not monopolise the favours of the bride until he had arranged for one of his friends to summon the bride and violate her. A bride might instead entrust her body to a man whom she liked or to an unmarried youth from among her relatives. Actions like these were probably vestiges of a 'first-night' custom.

In Aichi Prefecture, in the vicinity of Minami-shidara, some newlyweds made an offering of the first night to Ebisu, the God of Wealth. On the wedding day, Aichi brides might not exchange wine cups with the groom or the groom might be expected to vanish. In the midst of the first-night festivities, the groom might go with his friends to a brothel and remain there for several days. Giving 'the right of the first night' to a man other than the husband was euphemistically called 'a presentation to the gods'.

In earliest times, it was not the village youths who exercised first-night privileges but rather the village elder and sorcerer in overall charge of administration. Since the sorcerer was revered as an intermediary with the gods, presenting a virgin to him for defloration was considered the next best thing to having intercourse with a god. In some places, deflowering virgins was one of the emoluments of the matchmaker's office, with the matchmaker given the right to perform the sexual act with the bride as many as eight times. It appears that the first-night privilege was first entrusted to the gods and, finally, to the village youths who collectively possessed the girls in their villages.

The youths who regarded these girls as their own were ill disposed towards the young man who appeared ready to marry and monopolise one of them. So they took the girl's virginity; if the groom was an outsider, they further had a habit of direly inconveniencing him. In some places, the groom was forced to swallow fifteen or sixteen glasses of rice wine and many bowls of rice heaped to the brim. In other places, the just-married groom was denuded, placed in a mountain cart and conveyed to a nearby pond. While his captors harmonised musically with flutes and drums, the hapless groom was thrown into the middle of the pond. Teasing the groom in this way has continued, it is said, even into modern times.

During a first intercourse of newlyweds, the matchmaker might remain in close proximity to the couple, separated from them only by a screen. There he leisurely sipped his wine and patiently waited for evidence that the marriage had been consummated, signifying the successful completion of his mission. But if the inexperienced groom was unable to consummate the act, the matchmaker might then intrude upon the scene and deflorate the bride in the presence of the groom. The groom immediately benefited from this short but traumatic course in sex education, and from that point on was on his own.

HOLY TRANSMITTERS OF GODLY INTENT

The Shinto priests transmitted the intent of the gods to man and the requests of man to the gods. In places like Izumo's Senge, therefore, the priest himself was revered through the ages as a living god. The issue born to these living gods and the women such as shamanesses who served them were referred to as 'young princes'. There were, then, Shinto priests called gods to whom young virgins were offered. Pregnancy resulting from the union of a priest and a virgin was regarded as a great honour, with the infant referred to as a heaven-sent child of the gods. As late as 1875 and 1876, Shinto priests serving at a famous shrine in Ibaragi Prefecture would cover their faces with the mask of Tengu, the long-nosed goblin, and in this guise violate young girls. This practice may have been associated with a belief that the gods failed to respond when married couples visited the shrine and that it was best for women to attend alone. Defloration by the priest was an ancient prerogative accorded to him as a holy intercessor between man and the gods, and in places like Ibaragi it was observed until the present century.

OFFERING VAGINAS TO A STONE GOD

The Engaoka (Shinto) Shrine in Nagasaki Prefecture contains a stone statue shaped like a phallus. The night before a virgin was to get married, she would be brought to this shrine by her mother. There prayers were offered so that the bride-to-be might be blessed with sons. The white-clad Shinto priest who led the prayers then opened the doors to the inner stone shrine and reverently instructed the mother on how to sacrifice to the stone god. She in turn delivered her daughter to the god, with the girl assuming a seated position and opening her thighs. The humped-like tortoise head portion of the statue pressed against and rent her vagina, after which she rearranged her dress in the inner

47

recesses of the shrine.

This practice clearly was based on the concept that defloration was a right to be exercised by the gods. In some places, reference to this was couched in euphemistic terms: The virgin had 'stroked the god' or she had made 'a liquid offering to him', the latter reference presumably being to her having presented the god with the blood from her ruptured hymen. The custom of rupturing the hymen on a stone god was so deeply ingrained in places throughout Japan that it survived despite the strict regulatory actions that were initiated with the Meiji Restoration of 1868 to destroy lewd shrines and immoral practices, and there is evidence of its having been practised as late as the Taisho era (1912–25).

PREMARITAL SEX SEVERELY PUNISHED

The right of the first night was assumed in all instances in the belief that the girl was a virgin, with prior 'breaking of the melon' strictly forbidden. Citations from the Old Testament indicate that the compilers of the Bible judged the girl who had premarital relations to have lost her potential for marriage, and she could be stoned to death. One anthropologist theorised that hunters and farmers tolerated illicit intercourse before marriage but that nomadic peoples were extremely strict about chastity.

Eighth-century records in prose and poetry, however, reveal that Japanese women of earliest recorded history must have enjoyed a far greater degree of sexual freedom than did Japanese females of later centuries, during which religious-philosophical dogmas prevailed. The punishment of adultery and illicit intercourse in Japan was due mainly to the foreign influences of Buddhism and Confucianism. With the diffusion of foreign concepts of deity, the Japanese came to consider defilement of the gods a crime and sexual purity a matter of religious conviction. Women were even regarded as wives of the gods, and the blood from defloration was deemed holy. With these concepts in the background, there developed strict injunctions against a female's losing her purity before the wedding encounter.

VIII. Holy To Profane:
Priests, Pregnancy, Prostitutes

The ancient religion of Japan differed from Christianity in sexual outlook, for it did not denigrate women or regard sex as sinful or impure. In very old Japan, it was woman's task to serve the gods, with only virgins authorised to act as spiritual go-betweens. So the gods were surrounded by women, whose bodies could be enjoyed freely by the priests in charge. Pregnancy was then a divine mystery, and for the master priest to have sex with a mistress of the shrine was a holy matter of serving the gods. When such a mistress had a child from this union, she was revered as a 'god-mother' and the birth became a matter for communal celebration.

In ancient times, little distinction was made between prostitution, love, and marriage, and sex was regarded as neither impure nor criminal. The Sun Goddess of Japan's holy canon, a remote ancestor of the shamaness, on arriving late at Heaven's cliff-door thought nothing of stripping before the gods.

Through the medium of the shamaness, Japan's early prostitution came to be closely associated with the holy altar. There were two types of shamanesses, those serving in or near the palace and those serving at provincial shrines. In either case, they preceded the later development of the shamaness-prostitute. One text states, for example, that district shamanesses also rendered services as prostitutes. There were also harem service officers called *uneme* ('Court Maidens') recruited from earliest times, with many of them becoming beloved consorts of the emperors. The palace shamaness was offered up to the emperor by provincial governors and leading officials, while the provincial shamaness was selected from among the common people. The search was for beautiful and alluring virgins, some of whom were recruited from as far as neighbouring Korea.

An effort was made to maintain temple decorum. Pure women were exalted, defiled women could not serve the gods, and only the chief priest could have sex with the maidens. But rules became lax with the passage of time so that, starting with country and regional supervisors, powerful sponsors of the shrines came to usurp the same rights with the women that formerly the chief priests alone had enjoyed.

Many shamanesses who had finished serving the gods and had returned to their native villages attracted local males with their beauty and adopted a dual role of shamaness-prostitute. They also served at banquets. These women often lived near the palace on a fixed stipend, and they probably lived well. At least some of them had to lead chaste lives, for chastity was said to be a major qualification required of female wine servers. And males at the banquets who forced themselves upon them sexually were allegedly punished. Shrines were set up at important military, cultural, and economic centres, where it was natural for prostitutes to gather. So the association of shrine with prostitute and shamaness could not be eradicated. Prostitutes also used to attend festivals in droves, again because the shrine was the centre of commercial activity and a focal point for pleasure-seekers. With the outlawing of prostitution throughout Japan in April, 1958, brothel quarters are now prohibited, but the famous streets of commercial sex in the major cities all used to be located near the shrine areas.

Despite official efforts to legislate prostitution out of existence, if we define prostitution as receiving compensation for having sex with any well-to-do stranger or chance acquaintance, then it flourishes in modern Japan. The red-light districts have been silenced, it is true, but in the Yoshiwara area the role of the prostitute has been taken over by 'Miss *Toruko*',* the scantily-clad mistress of the baths who offers massage and a variety of services, the latter agreed upon through extensive negotiation. There are also hostesses, barmaids, and the occasional street-walker, proof that prostitution still exists, though in modified form. The interested male makes a quiet financial arrangement with the bar madam or the cabaret hostess, meets the woman later or escorts her then and there to an 'avec' inn. He can dally with her one or two hours or till the not-so-early morn, depending on the price he's paid. The street-walker in the large Japanese cities, however, is a much, much rarer phenomena than she is, for example, on one of the off-Broadway streets of New York. There are also no call-girls at the hotels and you have to go to the inn with a woman you've negotiated with on your own. This keeps the law-abiding innkeeper relaxed and happy, for the game is being played according to the rules.

The association of whore and altar goes back to remote antiquity and antedates Japanese practices by centuries. In Babylonia, for example, five centuries before the Christian era, brides-to-be had to sacrifice once before the holy altar to Venus, offering their

Toruko is the Japanese rendering of 'Turkish'.

50

bodies to strangers. Great numbers of them got together, hair bound in a special style with religious significance, hoping to be chosen by a man. None could return home until a man had tossed a few coins at her knees and had a night of sex with her. She could then unbind her hair, indicating she had fulfilled her obligations to the goddess, and depart. The ancient Japanese differed from the Babylonians in this respect, for to them only the special class of woman called 'the shamaness' was suited to serve the gods.

A special concept of virginity in ancient Japan arose from the belief that spirit and flesh could be restored through religious fasting. It was believed that, regardless of how many men with whom a woman had sex, if she menstruated her virginity was restored once the menstruation had ended. So in antiquity a virgin might be defined as an unmarried woman who was not yet pregnant, regardless of the state of her hymen.*

Prostitutes became socially recognised during the Nara era (eighth century). As has been shown, there were many prostitutes from antiquity onwards, but in quasi-religious roles. They did not form a distinct social class until the eighth century, when a class of prostitutes appeared which made its living solely from prostitution. The old term for lewd and dissolute women was *ukareme*, while a 'woman of play' was also called an *asobime*. The *asobime* of those times included shamanesses, dancing girls, and songstresses – in other words, women who had special knowledge and upbringing in religion, music, or even poetry. So, as was true of the upper-class courtesan in T'ang China (seventh to tenth centuries), their customers tended to be lords and high officials. These aristocratic customers spent large sums at feasts or gave other forms of compensation. When the *asobime* spent the night with them, some form of prostitution was involved, so the women sold their flesh as well as their talents. The aristocratic backgrounds of pre-Heian prostitutes was such that as a class they enjoyed a much higher social status than was true of later times. Women from fine families could become prostitutes, and they might be widely admired. The most highly revered prostitutes of the Heian era were the shamanesses and the nuns; by way of illustration there is on record an anecdote to the effect that the highly esteemed authoress Izumi Shikibu, unloved by her husband, went to a shamaness at one of the shrines in order to sell her love. The shamaness then exhibited her sex organs three times before the

*Ibid., p. 84. The author considers this concept superior to the present one in Japan of tolerating 'fake virgins with medically rebuilt hymens'. (The remains of the hymen are stitched together.)

god, but Izumi desisted from her quest because she was too embarrassed to do likewise. Here we see the shamaness as a holy matchmaker who sanctified the quest of a woman to engage in prostitution.

CHASTITY AND SLAVERY

The early dynastic eras were characterised by marriage based on choice – the so-called random marriage alluded to in our text. If a couple had sexual relations, they were considered married, but if they separated they reverted to single status. There was no question here of a viewpoint of chastity. If one felt an affinity for someone else, it was not improper to engage in sexual relations with that person.

Slavery existed in Japan from antiquity onwards, but laws to govern the system of slavery were not promulgated until the Nara era. The one enslaved, all human rights ignored, was bought and sold like a piece of property. Chastity for the slave, who might well be pawned, was never recognised. For example, if a debtor failed to pay back a loan, his wife and daughter could be turned over to the lender as collateral, to be used freely in sex until the debt was repaid. These women could also be made to perform work for the lender.

Local officials in charge of yearly tax collection could drag off as they pleased wives and daughters of men under their jurisdiction who failed to pay their taxes on time. Female slaves were usually more highly regarded than male slaves, and feminine beauty was negotiated for at very high prices. The woman's body could be used freely by her owner; wealthy and aristocratic families in the uppermost rung of the social ladder had as many as two to three hundred slaves. Slaves were not allowed to marry, and they were treated more like horses or dogs than like human beings.

PUNISHING THE SEXUAL TRANSGRESSIONS OF PRIESTS

Junshin was the famed lover-priest who left Godaisan Temple to break the commandments with Ouma, the daughter of a local tinsmith. They eloped but were later captured and sent into separate exile. Priests who indulged in sex with women were subject to much more severe punishment, but in the case of Junshin the

52

sentence was light because the shogunate system was coming to an end. In the Warring States period (late fifteenth to early sixteenth centuries), for example, priests were forbidden under penalty of death to go into homes where women lived alone. Women under fifty were also prohibited by one ruler, Nonaka Kenzan, to visit temples; in some of the temples, where women were kept out, homosexuality flourished.

The Buddha may have preached equality but, in the social context of the times, women came to be derided and abhorred. The anti-female attitude was especially evident in Japan, where woman was charged with being the root of sin and a fearful menace to a male-oriented society. 'Behind the incident there is a woman ...' 'outwardly a Bodhisattva, inwardly a she-devil.'* For more than a thousand years, from the spread of Buddhism and Confucianism to the intrusion of the Western world, Japanese women were looked down on as the personification of lewd desires. There was, for example, a folk saying to the effect that 'if you praise her, she becomes high handed. If you get angry with her, she cries. If you kill her, she comes back at night to haunt you.'

An effort was made to prohibit women from visiting certain mountain temples, part of an overall code of morals intended to remove temptation from the eyes of the priests. In 1406, a chief priest explicitly forbade the indulgence of priests in women, wine, and homosexuality. In 1525, even making a loud noise in the hot baths became a punishable offence. Later, the decrees were relaxed to the extent that cleaning women were allowed to work inside certain temples. But many priests associated carnally with these women and with women tilling the fields. Other priests got into the houses of ordinary women on the pretext of religious visits. These activities finally came to the attention of temple authorities.

The crime of fornication by priests might be dealt with by confinement, exile, or public ridicule. Priests in the Tokugawa era (1603–1867) who had relations with women were sentenced either to exile or exposure to public view. Sex with an unmarried girl was punished lightly, but having relations with another man's wife was regarded as a serious crime. Adultery was defined as having a woman stay in a monastery or a man stay in a nunnery. There are recorded allegations that in the early sixteenth century (1521–28) the activities of priests and nuns were extremely lewd. The head nun would get pregnant, it was charged, while rooms of

*Zankoku no Nihonshi, p. 218. Bodhisattva is one of the Buddhist terms for an enlightened religious person.

young nuns would be opened nightly to male visitors. Nuns and priests who broke the laws together were punished together. In the Tokugawa era, private whores might be referred to as *Bhiksuni,* a Sanskrit word for nuns, implying that nunnery and prostitution had come to be associated terms.

There was also considerable lesbianism, with harem ladies, nuns, and prostitutes buying and using masturbational implements. The widespread practice of lesbianism was such that one of the streets in the Yoshiwara brothel area specialised in women who could be approached by female customers only. Male homosexuality was forbidden to temple occupants as a violation of the religious commandments, but some priests did keep young boys, called 'catamites', for this purpose. While this practice is said to have got its start among Japanese priests, it gained momentum in the Warring States era through the erroneous application of military codes of morality and flourished in Tokugawa times among both the military and the townspeople. Many fictional works dating from the Tokugawa era idealise male prostitution. Women *kabuki* players were banned in 1629 as being injurious to the maintenance of public morality, and the men who replaced them prospered in a dual role as actors by day and prostitutes by night. In 1648, the shogunate prohibited male prostitution, and in the summer of that year it placed a ban on *kabuki* plays as well. But two of the shoguns were homosexually inclined, the third shogun at first ignoring women in favour of men and the fifth shogun owning 150 catamites. In 1667, calling at the temples by actors and dancers was expressly prohibited, but until the Meiji era male prostitution was a factor in Japanese society not to be ignored. Male prostitutes were treated as an inferior class, restricted to living in certain areas and forbidden from 1688 on to be transported on horses or in palanquins. Other men, who were not kabuki actors, made a living from prostitution as a regular trade.

Their way of life resembled that of female whores and they usually originated from poor townspeople or dispossessed samurai. They were taught to play musical instruments, serve tea, and play Japanese chess, and from the age of fourteen or fifteen they began to receive customers. Wooden implements, first small and then increasing in size, were inserted into the anus until it could accommodate the penis of a customer without experiencing pain or inflammation. Various oils and medicines were applied to facilitate this objective.

Male whores used lipstick, eyebrow colouring, red and white

powder, and a variety of the cosmetics then in use by women, trying to achieve the same genteel feminine effect. Only their dress and hair style remained masculine. They were usually in their teens, although there is a reference to a youthful-looking male prostitute who stayed in the business until middle age. Once they became professionals, they were subject to cruel mistreatment for refusing customers. They might be hung upside down from the rafters, pierced on the arms or buttocks with sewing needles. While they were working, very special attention was given to what they ate to ensure that they did not become constipated. They avoided ill-smelling foods and took scrupulous care of their skins.

Many famous tea houses on Yedo streets served as places of assignation, some flourishing till the end of the shogunate period. One writer of the times referred to 220 male prostitutes, but the actual number must have been much greater. They tended to work near famous shrines, luring such customers as priests, samurai, and playboys. Guests in the tea houses followed the same formalities as in engaging women, usually contracting for one to two hours. The custom of male prostitution diminished with the Meiji Restoration and it is illegal and rare in modern Japan.

IX. Chastity and the Double Standard

The Japanese story of creation refers to one male, Izanagi, and one female, Izanami, but from pre-Heian times (ca. seventh century) polygamy was practised by anyone who desired more than one wife and could afford the upkeep. A decree of the Taiho era (701–4) stipulated three women (for one man) – two levels of wives and a concubine – and another decree concerned with taking care of the aged listed within its provisions one wife and one concubine. The Heian era recognised three levels of wives and a plurality of concubines, setting forth a system of polygamy which was practised in a modified way until the dawn of the modern era. Polygamy has been a far more common phenomenon in the world than polyandry, with the man being allowed many wives because of the importance attached in a patrilineal society to the preservation of his lineage. It was common for a man to be allowed concubines under the rationalisation of lineage, but a woman was strictly forbidden to have sexual relations with any male other than her husband. Therefore, chastity in this context proved to be a man-made restraining device imposed on women to assure that they remained servile to the male. In Japan, following the lead of its Confucian Chinese neighbour, it was said from antiquity that 'a chaste woman does not have two husbands'. Women were forcibly dissuaded from marrying a second time, with the Taiho and 'old-age provision' decrees sentencing a woman to exile for one year if she married while in mourning for a deceased husband. But no questions were asked of the husband who remarried after his wife died. The ancient Hindu religion was much harsher in its requirement that widows be sacrificed to enable them to keep their husbands company in death. In the Yedo era (1603–1867), when her husband died the wife was encouraged to vow fidelity to the deceased for the rest of her life. If she did, she received a posthumous name which symbolised virtuous widowhood. This made it exceedingly difficult for the Japanese widow to ever re-wed. The Confucian-indoctrinated male aversion to marrying widows and divorcees has continued into modern times, so that today far fewer women in these categories remarry than they do in the West. Back in the Yeda era, it was customary to prepare a joint grave, linking the names of husband and wife for eternity. Child brides among the aristocracy were not uncommon; when Shogun Ietsugu died in childhood at the age of eight, his infant bride was three years old. She received a lifetime rice allowance from the shogunate, preserving her virginity in chaste solitude until she died in her mid-forties. As in imperial China, chastity was demanded even of the fiancée, who by Yedo law was subject to punishment as an adulteress if she had relations with someone other than her affianced. If her fiancé died, she was not allowed to marry but instead was morally and legally forced to remain a virgin. However, in actual practice so many sex-starved or economically pressed widows turned to prostitution that the term 'widow' itself came to be used as a euphemism for 'whore'. Some found an outlet through lesbianism and used masturbational devices, following the pattern of nuns and harem women. Various kinds of phallic devices were sold in the market place, known by names such as 'single enjoyment' and 'the laughing tool'. They were penis-shaped, made of water buffalo horn, tortoise shell, or metal, and first warmed in hot water before using. There was also a sexual tool available for lesbian partners to use at the same time. The public display and sale of phallic devices was prohibited in 1804 and in 1842, but they continued to be secretly sold.

Powerful clans in Japan tried to arrange marriages with the imperial clan from the time of Emperor Nintoku (313–99) on. There was the so-called Court Maiden, similar to the official prostitute employed by the Koreans. She seems to have been recruited at first solely to serve the gods, but after the Taiho era (701–4) it was decreed that she serve in one of thirteen offices within the confines of the palace. These women, who also supervised the royal kitchens, rendered services to the emperor and, on occasion, were loaned to foreign envoys. The Court Maiden served the gods and their holy representative, the emperor, who recruited her by lineage and appearance. She gave birth to imperial sons and figured in palace intrigues and disputes over succession to the throne.

The Fujiwara clan, which dominated the late Heian scene, sent women into the imperial harem and gained power through a network of wife-concubine liaisons. The clan used its women to attain political objectives and to get powerful rivals expelled from the palatial centre of influence. With the passage of time, political marriages became a sort of human sacrifice in which women were coercive victims. Toyotomi Hideyoshi (late sixteenth century) forbade such marriages in an effort to prevent feudal lords from fomenting alliances, but his political rival Tokugawa Ieyasu managed nevertheless to marry these daughters into three powerful clans. But when Ieyasu gained power, he strictly guarded against politically-motivated marriages, meanwhile making further marital alliances for his clan alone.

COURT MAIDENS

Both East and West have known the practice of offering up wives and daughters to those in power for the protection and glory of the male householder. This was an extremely precious gift, given in eras in which a woman's chastity was valued as more resplendent than gold. The custom may have originated as a human sacrifice, in which a live victim was offered to the god to assure his patronage and blessings. Whatever the origin, there are references in connection with the Taika Reform of 645 to the beautiful female officials called *uneme* ('Court Maidens'). This female attendant came from the provinces to live in the court, with her living expenses defrayed by the province. Later, the central government did provide for her food, but nothing more. Her living and clothing expenses were assumed by her parents and elder brothers, and she was despatched to court service without the recompense of the court. But her father and elder brother at the very least strengthened their local official positions, and they benefited from behind the scenes for having offered the girl to the court as a kind of sacrifice of the flesh. This was the awesome fate to which she was at first consigned. Of course, the wit and beauty of such women provided them with special opportunities for advancement, for as female court official attending to the emperor's needs they enjoyed a special status. Even ministers had to maintain a respectful distance from them, while on their part they could not show the slightest interest in a man other than the emperor. It is alleged that at a wine feast given by Emperor Yuryaku (reigned 456–79) one of these girls was threatened with decapitation merely for having let the leaf of a tree drop into the wine she was serving. She finally escaped execution through a song in which she pleaded for her life. She symbolised in the extreme the fate of traditional Japanese women, who had to endure life as playthings of the male. Women, it was said, might be placed on imperial view while being forced to participate in nude female wrestling matches. For political expediency or financial gain, innumerable beauties were forced into marriages dictated by strategy. These included the daughters of feudal lords, warlords, landowners, and tenant farmers.

WIVES FOR THE NIGHT

In Japan, from antiquity to the Middle Ages, certain women married to beaucrats were given assignments as 'female officers for the night'. When a high-ranking Japanese was despatched from the central government to the distant provinces, the wife or daughter at the home of the local official where he was staying would serve him till the dawn. This was considered natural hospitality, although viewed in a different perspective it would seem to violate Confucian family and chastity concepts. If the wife and daughter refused to submit to the stranger, the local official involved could be dismissed or demoted. The custom of having 'wives for the night', therefore, came into being through the establishment and maintenance of a powerful central authority. In one instance dating back to the Heian period, the husband not only ordered his wife to serve the visiting dignitary but also made the same demand of her thirteen-year-old sister. But the wife resisted strongly, and when night fell she alone made herself available to the guest. This practice did not represent a simple folk custom for entertaining the traveller but was rather a fixed pattern of behaviour decreed for a double-standard society, with the wife's spirit and flesh used to enhance the husband's glory and well-being.

FEMALE PAWNS IN POLITICAL MARRIAGES

The nobles during the Warring States era (late fifteenth century) considered it proper to force their daughters into politically-contrived weddings. Such marriages were pacts between two powerful forces; if the forces, however, had a falling-out, either partner to the marriage might become a hostage. The famed shogun Oda Nobunaga was a master at using the technique of political marriage. He himself married the daughter of a man whom he later eliminated, and he arranged marriages for three of his sons in such a way that they were adopted into three powerful clans. (In Japan, to the present day the male may be adopted upon marriage into his wife's clan, whereupon he assumes his wife's maiden name.) Nobunaga also had his daughter Oichi marry Asai Nagamasa; with the annihilation of Asai, she was then forced to marry Shibata Katsuie. As Shibata died, Oichi decided that two forced marriages were enough for one lifetime and she stabbed herself to death. Toyotomi Hideyoshi had his younger sister join the house of Tokugawa Ieyasu, the great founder of the Tokugawa hegemony, and through marriage alliances developed an intricate group of influential in-laws.

Such marriage pacts could be dissolved as circumstances dictated, resulting in great suffering to the wife-made-pawn, since one part of her ideological upbringing was to pay at least lip service to the theory of chastity and fidelity to one man alone. When Ukita Naoie, for example, attacked the walled city of Takada in 1565, he made off with the mayor's wife. At his death, his son presented this woman to Hideyoshi, who became inordinately fond of her. As a result, Naoie's son was made a Grand General, though still a youth in his early twenties. There were countless stories like this. One widower, a Catholic, was ordered by his father to marry. He complained that he had been victimised by the family system and for the rest of his life abstained from having sexual relations with his second wife.

59

The history of divorce in Japan makes clear the extent to which the feelings of the woman were ignored. There are references to divorce in the myths of the eighth century *Kojiki* ('Chronicle of Ancient Events'), but the earliest historical evidence is in the Taiho era (701–4) *Regulations*. Four types of divorce were set forth:

1. Agreement.
2. Legal compulsion.
3. Losing all trace of the other partner.
4. Unilateral abandonment of the wife by the husband.

The Japanese followed a strictly Chinese system of Confucian ethics when they promulgated the 'seven expulsions'. A husband had seven options for getting rid of his wife, namely: barrenness; adultery; disobedience to her in-laws; loquaciousness; theft; jealousy; malignant disease.

In the Warring States period (1482–1588), divorce usually resulted in boys going with the father and girls with the mother. The Yedo shogunate (1603–1867) strictly decreed divorce for women who drank a great amount of tea and enjoyed leisurely frolics in the mountains. A divorce paper consisting of three and one-half lines of a fixed Japanese format was presented to the wife's parents. The wife could not remarry without it, and without it she could be incriminated for adultery if she had relations with a man other than her husband. The divorce paper bluntly stated that the man had divorced his wife and made it clear that henceforth he severed all relations with her. Consisting of only three and a half lines (half the length of the seven-line marriage document), it stated: 'You and I are free to do as we please, so from now on we are divorced (literally, 'separated from affinities'). Therefore, hereafter each of us can marry again with whoever we choose. May there be no hindrance to this nor any confining stipulation.' (Followed by the date, the man's name and his seal, and then the woman's name.) The man could either write it himself or have it written for him. It was the only acceptable legal proof of divorce. The man had to hand the divorce paper to his wife or to her parents. If he remarried without it, he could be exiled from his village, while the wife in like circumstance was forcibly tonsured and sent back to her parents. As was true of the Chinese and Koreans, it was extremely difficult for the wife to get a divorce, virtually impossible without the husband's consent, despite justification or circumstance. Everything was weighted in favour of the man. In a few places, however, there were temples to which the estranged wife could flee and, after staying there for a fixed amount of time, be granted a divorce. The Tokeji Temple in Northern Kamakura, which flourishes to the present day, was famous for this practice. After Hojo Tokimune's wife became an imperial priestess, in order to rescue wives from the cruelty of their mates she allowed them to be divorced from their husbands if they had lived alone in Tokeji Temple for three years. In Nitta, Gumma Prefecture, women who stayed at Mantokuji Temple (which had close connections with the Tokugawa family) for three years and then sent their husbands a few strands of hair from their heads were recognised as divorced. But during those three years they could not leave the temple; while their hair was unshorn, they still had to conduct themselves like nuns. It was said that they were not at all distressed, since they could move about in the temple as they pleased. Also, there were apparently samurai stationed at the temple gates to prevent irate husbands from seizing their wives and forcing them to return home. But these temples of mercy and refuge were not sanctioned everywhere. In the Sendai region at Date, the flight of a wife to a temple or any other site was prohibited, and all such escapees were returned to their husbands. Not until 1873 was a woman allowed to petition legally to be granted a divorce.

The Japanese wife from antiquity onwards had to serve her husband with exclusive devotion. It was the wife who trembled in fear and uneasiness, for she had no recourse if her husband decided to take a concubine or to abandon or divorce her.

X. Sexual Outlook, Era by Era

LOVE EXCHANGES IN THE NARA ERA

In the Nara era (710–795), the man would go at night to the room of his wife or his lover, returning to his own quarters with the dawn. It was an age prior to venereal disease, an age in which pleasures were shared freely. The man would send love poems to move the heart of his beloved. These women, as in modern India, generally lived in the recesses of the home, rarely going out of doors. Even when they did, they would ride in a screened carriage or cover their faces with a veil. To discover if she was really beautiful, a man had to embrace a woman with open eyes. The men of the age expressed love sentiments through song and thereby gained their love objectives. The nights were so dark that men often embraced unattractive females. Unlike the modern Japanese, men and women did not frequent the hot baths, so dirt must have accumulated on all of them, even women of good families. Upper-class women used perfumes, but the odour of the men they were with must have lingered for several days – by modern standards, their sexual exchanges were quite unsanitary.

People of the Nara era did not change into bedclothes but slept in whatever they were wearing. The doll illustrations of that early age show that they used a kind of *tatami* matting, not a very satisfactory type of sleeping accommodation. They had neither cushions nor sheets, and the woman could not spread a new *tatami* mat in anticipation of the man's arrival. They ate in their rooms, so the odour of food must also have lingered. Paper was then very expensive and many could not afford it, so perhaps when intercourse ended they did not clean themselves at all or wiped themselves with cloth.

HEIAN HEDONISM

The Heian age lasted four hundred years, from the transfer of the capital from Nara to Heiankyo (modern Kyoto) in the late eighth century to the establishment of a shogunate at Kamakura four centuries later. The upper classes of the Heian age generally pursued fleeting pleasures and were addicted to sensual delights. A class of prostitutes (still called *ukareme*) flourished, and what has been called 'boudoir government' prevailed, based on the matrimonial influences exerted on the throne by one branch of the Fujiwara clan. The Fujiwara clan thrived on successful harem manoeuvres, until after six generations one of its branches seized power. Fujiwara Michinaga, head of one branch of the clan, married five daughters to four emperors and an heir apparent, respectively, and Michinaga wielded authority as the grandfather of three emperors. So one might even call the history of the Heian era a history of the rise and fall in the fortunes of one branch of the Fujiwara clan. This group succeeded because of its strategic and dominant position as the only family providing the royal house with outsiders.

The way to influence the throne was through having one's daughter accepted into the imperial harem. If she was favoured by the emperor, her father and brothers became influential, even more so if she gave birth to the son who became an heir apparent. So there was much jealousy and intrigue in the harem – it was unavoidable.

Pretty young Heian women did not bother to remain virgins until they married but instead went from one man to another, loving, dissolving the union, and loving again. Men in power had many wives and concubines, and mothers and sons-in-law might even sleep together. Uncles and nieces and brothers and sisters had incestuous relations, and officials had amorous contacts with harem ladies in broad daylight. Fujiwara Yukinari liked to look into the rooms of harem wives when they were just waking from sleep, saying that was when they were most appealing.

THE HEIAN FEMALE DISPOSITION

Lacking a concept of chastity, Heian women tended to be flighty. Love could be mutually unresponsive. A woman might not love someone but she would be praised for her compassion if she had sexual intercourse with him. Relations between men and women were unstable. A couple would unite for the moment, but they disliked enduring relationships. They married casually and often, and by the age of thirty were considered prematurely aged because of their excessive indulgence in promiscuous sex.

A TYPICAL HEIAN MALE

Arihara no Narihira symbolised the easy-going voluptuary so prevalent during the Heian age. He was talented and handsome, a libertine who visited different women night after night. According to one text, the stories of love in the pre-tenth century *Ise Monogatari* were inspired by Arihira's real-life conduct. He exchanged vows, it is said, with 3,333 women. (The number here is one of great significance to the male, for in the Chinese Taoist numerology known to Heian males, three was a number with great male potency.) But only twelve of the beautiful women with whom Arihara was intimate were actually described. The number

3,333 is undoubtedly exaggerated, and one chosen for its numerological significance,* but it gives us some idea of what was considered the potential for free involvements in the Heian age.

TYPICAL HEIAN WOMEN

There were many women writers; to gain prominence, a woman had to be not only attractive but accomplished in poetry or prose. Women were loved by Heian aristocrats for their feminine charms and the delicate ways in which they communicated emotions. Foremost among such women was Ono Komachi, an unparalleled beauty and a poetic genius. One official made love to her for ninety-nine days and then died of exhaustion. Miss Ono was said to have tired of a succession of lovers. Her case was typical, for almost all of the foremost women of the Heian age practised diversity in sexual relations. The novelist Murasaki Shikibu was an exception – she married only once, remaining chaste after her husband died. But the literary lady Izumi Shikibu mentioned previously had marital and extramarital sex with many men. Diarist Sei Shonagon was not known for her physical charms, and none of her male acquaintances had enduring affairs with her.

Lady Murasaki's *Tales Of Genji* reveals that beautiful women of lowly birth could become imperial favourites. This book (translated into English by Arthur Waley) was written in an age of sexual hedonism. Genji had many complex love relations. At twelve, he was put through a ceremony for attaining manhood called *gempuku*, in which he changed his hair style and adopted the style of dress of an adult, wearing a headdress for the first time. Since Genji was the emperor's favourite son, he was given a resplendent ceremony. He was very handsome, and to show his appreciation he performed a dance at court so esthetically that it brought tears to the emperor's eyes.

It was arranged for Genji to bed that night with an official's daughter, a custom called 'supplementary lying down' observed by heirs apparent and princes when they completed the capping ceremony. However, when the 'lying down' ceremony was proposed, young Genji was embarrassed and he failed to respond. But that night he was entertained at the mansion of the Great Minister on the Left, who bestowed on him a teenage daughter. She can therefore be regarded as Genji's first wife.

Completion of the capping ceremony by the youth signified he

*Cf. Ishihara and Howard S. Levy, *The Tao of Sex*, p. 4.

was ready to undertake the responsibilities of politics and marriage. He usually married soon afterwards. When it became public knowledge that a prince was ready for the ceremony, aristocrats with comely daughters of marriageable age offered them as brides.

Heian women also went through a kind of puberty rite when they were considered to have reached adulthood. Japanese today are welcomed into the adult fold at twenty, but for the Heian female the age was between twelve and fourteen, slightly later for the male. So the ancients must have regarded emerging sexuality as the key to adulthood. The woman then for the first time wore a special dress and bound her hair in a special style. From that time on the strands of hair which had been draped around the shoulders were rearranged in an upwards fashion. It was then felt to be immodest for a woman to look directly at any man other than her husband, so the lustrousness of her hair afforded the first hint to the male admirer of her prospective beauty. In an age of physical concealment, therefore, much more attention was given to the way a woman dressed her hair. When she aged or got seriously sick, the woman might leave her home and go to a temple in order to plan for her exit from this life and her ascendance to the Buddhist paradise known as the Pure Land. She became a nun, as did rejected lovers, not tonsuring the hair to a state of baldness but rather cutting it so that instead of coursing down the length of her body it now ended at her shoulders.

As alluded to above, women of the aristocratic class in the Heian age didn't show their faces to men other than their husbands. Even the prospective husband (as was true of many traditional Chinese) didn't see his bride's face until after the marriage – what a traumatic experience that must have been! Heian stories revealed how anxiety-ridden males explored every chance to catch a glimpse of the woman unawares, to avoid a lifetime of chagrin and melancholy. The woman sometimes allowed this by rolling up the screen behind which she was concealed or by strolling into the garden where she could be observed. Covert meetings of the enamoured, with the man surreptitiously climbing over a wall and into his lovely neighbour's garden, form poetic episodes in both Chinese and Japanese literature, with empassioned lovers thus defying the institutional rigidities imposed by society and the elders who ruled it.

Prior to the eighth century, when the Japanese married, the male presented gifts to his betrothed and made further bestowals at the time of the wedding. The bride appeared at a table laden with food and drink, waiting on the groom. But formal marriage ceremonies were probably not entered into until about the mid-tenth century. These celebrations came to be called 'the rice-cakes for three days and three nights'.

Marriage in early Japan could be initiated through mutual love, with the man going nightly to the woman's home. There he might stay overnight to have intercourse regularly with her. This form of marriage emphasised the woman's family more than the man's, for it was the girl's parents who first recognised the marital state. 'New pillow' was the name given to this custom of encouraging a man to go to the home of his beloved to share the night with her; after three days and three nights the girl's parents apparently accepted him as their son-in-law. Their marriage being accepted, the couple ate cakes together, the so-called rice-cakes for three days and three nights. These cakes were the antecedents of the modern wedding cake that bride and groom cut and eat together.

The custom of the cakes is described in detail in the old story called *Ochikubo monogatari* ('The Tale of Ochikubo'), which implies that someone, not directly related to the couple had to make the cakes, of which there were two types. The hero of our story claimed that, being a bachelor, he still didn't know how to eat the cakes. But he finally ate three of them. By the Muromachi era (mid-fourteenth century), the system of the cakes was replaced by one in which bride and groom exchanged wine-cups 'three-times-three' or nine times. The cakes were no longer eaten; instead they were placed in the bedroom for three days, after which they were buried in the garden.*

The East Asia of antiquity was a region of poets. In Japan, as in other Asian countries, the man who had spent the night with a woman was expected to reveal his sentiments to her delicately through poetry and prose. It was essential that he write well. As we see in 'The Tale of Ochikubo', a less-gifted suitor might ask a skilled writer to compose a love poem for him.

If husband and wife quarrelled, the woman could tell the man to get out, the exact reverse of contemporary practice. The woman of antiquity was the central figure within the home, for in those days it was the man who left home to marry. So he had to depend on his wife's family for a place to stay.

Prostitution in Japan flourished in this era. The ageing shamanesses who fell out of favour moved about freely, selling their bodies to the highest bidder. There were also Buddhist nuns who

*Wakamori Taro, *Onna no issho* ('Woman's Life'), Kawade snobo shinsha, Tokyo, 1964, p. 87.

66

emulated their Shinto sisters in this regard. Under the pressures of war and privation, destitute families were forced to sell their daughters in order to survive. And the side defeated in war might also have to sell its daughters to the victors. The military class arose; facing death in the morning, they hastened to purchase women for the night. Supply kept pace with demand. The presence of whores in the army camps is shown by the statement in one text that when official troops attacked, many women were discovered at the enemy's camp. The night before that last battle, warriors might be embraced by dozens of beautiful women. There were many different names for prostitutes, ranging from elaborate words for palace concubines to plainer words for commoners. Women wandered about in gypsy-like troupes, displaying their artistic talents and selling their bodies. The highest class of prostitutes associated only with aristocrats; others achieved fame as dancers.

THE AGE OF THE WARRIOR

The low status of the military changed for the better towards the end of the Heian era (late twelfth century). And in the thirteenth and fourteenth centuries, during the Kamakura era, they surged to prominence. The marriage system, heretofore one in which the family selected a husband for the daughter, shifted in the opposite direction, so that the family chose a bride for the son. The military, being strong willed, hated defeat. They rejected the softness and compassion of the Heian age, and they tended towards coolness and lack of sentiment (or an overt display of it) in human relations. Fighting men faced with an uncertain future surrounded themselves with women and discouraged enduring one-to-one unions. It was a more barbaric world, one in which Heian elegance could not survive. With the military boasting of their strong wills, a fierce and unyielding kind of love became the norm. Political marriages flourished, with many women of the Kamakura age sacrificed to political objectives. It was during this age that the woman began to move to the husband's home after the marriage. But this was only true of the military class; the aristocratic groom still joined the family of the bride. Unlike the present system in Japan of the 'adopted son', the male of this era never assumed the identity of the wife's clan but kept his own identity.

It has often been said that in the East families marry, not individuals, and this was certainly true of the Kamakura era.

Women were betrothed in their early teens; there are even records of girls being betrothed or sent into the imperial harem at the age of nine. These children were contracted for in name only, and there were no sexual acts involved. The object was to unite influential families, and the feelings of the child-bride and groom were ignored. In some cases men and women were forced by their parents to divorce and marry someone else.

Some exquisite Kamakura women became renowned for skill in dancing and singing; far superior in attainment to ordinary women, they were well received by the upper class.

Kamakura prostitutes worked under official auspices. In about 1261, a tax was levied on these women, legally recognised as affording solace to military men who could not afford to be accompanied by their wives.

THE MUROMACHI ERA (1338–1573)

In this era, women were bought and sold like articles of personal property or presented to friends. This is quite reminiscent of how the Chinese treated prostitutes during the T'ang dynasty (seventh to tenth centuries A.D.).* Merchants who bought and sold human beings achieved prominence in the Muromachi era, an era also characterised by the spread of public gambling and private prostitution.

Prostitutes were sold this way at the end of the Kamakura era, and by the Muromachi era this became a thriving enterprise. There was very little government control – girls were subject to sale, rape, and seizure. (The prize-winning film *Rasshomon* mirrors one aspect of this age.) There were no state laws to protect the poor and the weak, and trade in human flesh flourished. There was thievery everywhere, officials worked primarily for their own selfish ends, and yearly tribute failed to be delivered to the capital. The situation at court became so acute that one diarist there described how he had to forsake breakfast and pawn the clothes he had received from the emperor in order to survive. The Ashikaga government squandered money on mansions and indulged in wine, women, and song. As they used up their funds, they resorted to heavy taxation of the people, which included taxing prostitutes. One ruler was assisted in his lewd pleasures by more than forty attendants; he dragged an official's mother into his bedroom, to share her there with his son. Also inclined towards homo-

*Howard S. Levy, *T'ang Women of Pleasure*, Sinologica (1965), 2, pp. 89–114.

sexuality, he finally spent so much money that he could not even afford the expenses of childbearing for a beloved concubine. To secure the needed gold he had to pawn helmets and spears. The son who joined with him in amorous play became impotent through over-indulgence. Another ruler severely penalised illicit behaviour, but he was killed before this could have much lasting effect.

NUDE PARTIES JAPANESE-STYLE

During this era there were special parties in which all the men took off their clothes. Girls in their late teens, wearing only one thin silk garment, poured the wine. There might be about twenty such women in attendance, whose beautiful skins showed through the sheer dresses. Women then wore no undergarments, so their figures were as fully revealed as if they had been standing in the nude. This kind of nude party must have been the ultimate in seductive excitement for the times.

The shoguns (military rulers) indulged in profligate behaviour, and their subordinates followed suit. One subordinate, secretary to an Ashikaga, raped the wives of other men, including high officials, and was officially involved with six thousand women! He appropriated every beauty in the area under his jurisdiction and summoned the wives of retainers into his bedroom, one by one, to 'flavour them'.

WOMEN AS SEXUAL PAWNS: THE MOMOYAMA ERA (1576–98)

The Momoyama era marked a reversion to earlier hedonistic practices, with women exploited for sexual and political purposes. One warrior, for example, typical of that age, arranged for one of his daughters to marry feudal leader Oda Nobunaga to forge a political alliance. Many others did likewise; there were numerous marriages based on political expediency rather than morality or love. Women of this epoch lived tragic lives, pawns in the struggle for political power. Regardless of her pedigree or her beauty, the woman was regarded simply as an instrument for achieving official ambitions and objectives.

Oda Nobunaga's relations with women were not especially notable, perhaps because he died at the age of forty-nine, an age at which he might otherwise have gained further sexual momentum. He is best known as a lover through his homosexual relations with a beautiful male youth. But his successor Hideyoshi was very active sexually, possessing many women even while his predecessor Nobunaga was still alive. Hideyoshi's wife once wrote a letter to Nobunaga, complaining of her husband's unrestrained sex life. After Nobunaga died, Hideyoshi became even freer in his sexual pursuits, accumulating five wives. They were all young, about the age of his children. Hideyoshi was of a lower-class background but he liked upper-class women, and he refused to have anything to do with women of the lower class no matter how beautiful they were. He was a fancier of the boudoir, a boudoir shared with more than thirty concubines of distinguished lineage. The feudal lords contemporary with Hideyoshi were also sexually indulgent. When ships came into Japan from the south, conveying bearers of venereal disease, prostitutes spread the disease through Japan and the feudal lords contracted it. Hideyoshi's close advisor Kuroda had it, and one of Tokugawa Ieyasu's sons lost part of his nose as a result of it. When the son put on a false nose to conceal the shame and embarrassment that he felt, Ieyasu criticised him, noting that samurai never covered up their features or paid attention to them. When part of his nose dropped off, concluded Ieyasu, his son never should have tried to conceal his looks.

ORIGIN OF THE PROSTITUTION DISTRICTS

Hara Saburo, one of Hideyoshi's favourite warriors, had to retire because of bodily injuries. He lived in a small hut, with his military weapons placed outside the door. Hideyoshi once passed by this hut and, discovering that it belonged to Hara, felt very sorry for him. He therefore gave him permission to set up a brothel district. Hara surmised that Hideyoshi would be pleased if it became a busy and prosperous place, for this would afford a distraction from military pursuits and so mean peace for the nation. Therefore he and a friend at once opened several brothels. Hideyoshi then advised that it would be best to have the houses side by side, so that all prostitutes could be assembled in one place. There were at first only a few brothels in the area. Adorned by willow trees on both sides, the street came to be called either 'The Place of Willows and Horses' or 'The Willow Amusement Quarters'. Authorities felt that the quarters were too close to the imperial residence, so in later years they were twice forced to move.

This was how the publicly recognised prostitution quarters got their start. Other quarters sprung up in imitation, and a few decades later there were such quarters all over Japan.

XI. Sex and the Shoguns

The Yedo era, also called the Tokugawa era, was most inauspicious for Japanese women. In the aftermath of more than two centuries of war and uprising, Tokugawa Ieyasu established his shogunate at Yedo (the Tokyo area). The unhappy state of the Japanese female worsened, for the start of the era was marked by social unrest; families were severed and lands were seized by force. The Tokugawa rulers publicly recognised concubines and led the way by keeping some themselves. Tokugawa Ieyasu, the famous founder of the dynasty that ruled Japan until the coming of the West, had nine concubines, 'nine' incidentally being the highest number of male potency.* Subordinates were allowed few women, but plurality in the name of perpetuating the clan was a doctrine prevalent among the *daimyo*, the term used to designate feudal lords.

So the man of rank and lineage took a wife in order to beget heirs. She was expected to be submissive, not to become jealous no matter how many other wives her husband had, and to advise him to take another woman if she thought that woman had qualities that she lacked. Such was the fate of the Yedo wife. Sexual instructions for the boudoir explicitly advised against the male's having intercourse with any female over thirty,† and this aspect of the instructions was scrupulously followed. When a shogun's wife passed thirty, it was believed that her potential for pregnancy was greatly lowered, and she was ordered to keep out of the boudoir. A young woman then came on the scene as a replacement. This must have been a welcome regulation for the

---

*According to the Chinese Taoist ideology that permeated the boudoir. *The Tao of Sex*, p. 4.
†Boudoir philosophers spurned the woman over thirty. (Ibid., p. 24.)

71

passionate, double-standard male to implement, and in the shogun's harem quarters known as the Great Inner Harem it was practised on a wide scale.

Several hundred women spent a life-long captivity in the shogun's harem, the shogun having complete control over their lives. For him it was a kingdom of sex, an island of women for whom contact with the outside world had been severed. Under the pretext of ensuring heirs for him, women who pleased the shogun's eye were taken continuously into his harem, regardless of social status. The organisation of the shogun's harem was vast and complex, with more than two hundred rooms of varying sizes. These were divided into two sections, the Middle Inner and the Great Inner, with the shogun the only man living there. Like the ancient Chinese emperors, whose harem organisations served as models, the shoguns observed a strict hierarchy in the ranks of harem women. Their women ranged in age and position from seven elders to more than a hundred young attendants. There were more than three hundred harem designees and, taking into account the domestic and kitchen help, the total number of women employed in boudoir or other tasks came to about five or six hundred. A weak man would have perished in their midst, but rigor in the boudoir was the mark of the Yedo shoguns. They were not especially long lived, but the main reason for this was not so much sexual dehabilitation as the contraction of contagious diseases which, lacking concepts of sanitation, they were powerless to prevent. The yearly expenses for this resplendent harem were estimated at two billion yen (about fifty-five million dollars!).

The shogun's boudoir was most unusual, arranged in a manner inconceivable to the modern mind. A female working there, who could be as young as twelve or thirteen, was referred to as an 'honourable small surname'.* She served an apprenticeship by first waiting on ladies of noble lineage, providing them with tobacco and with water for washing their hands. She was also called an 'honourable closemouth'. She tinkled a bell to announce the arrival of the shogun's messenger, who would inform an elderly woman in administrative charge of the Great Inner that the shogun wished to spend the night with a particular concubine. Then began the thorough preparation for having this concubine attend the shogun. She was made to wait in a small room for as long as an hour while various maids readied her for the occasion. The elder in charge let down the girl's hair to make sure that no

*When she became sixteen or seventeen, her designation was changed to 'honorable middle surname'.

72

weapons – or anything else, for that matter – had been concealed in her tresses.

When the shogun arrived, the chief elder had one of her assistants serve him tea. They chatted for a little while, after which he retired. But the shogun and his favourite-for-the-night could not share the intimacy of the covers in whispered privacy, for there were two other women in the bedroom in addition to the woman with whom he had sexual intercourse. One was considerably advanced in years. Her head was shaved and she was called the 'fairy monk'. The other woman, much younger, was called a 'bed supplement'. She arranged the shogun's night toilette and remained awake throughout the night. Perhaps it was feared that she would become diverted from her duties because of sexual arousal as she heard the sounds and movements of love; at any rate, we are informed that she swallowed in advance a certain medicine intended to act as an emotional depressant, an aphrodisiac in reverse. This woman was probably assigned to the bedroom to ensure that the shogun's concubine-for-the-night did not take advantage of sexual intimacy for making personal or political solicitations. So the 'bed supplement' had to listen carefully to every word that was uttered.

The shogun's bedding was first spread in the centre of the bedroom, with that of the concubine to his right. Separated somewhat from him and to his left was the bedding of the 'bed supplement'. And to the right of the shogun's companion, again somewhat separated from her, was the bedding of the 'fairy monk', who likewise remained awake and diligent until the dawn. So the four of them lay down in the boudoir of the Great Inner, head alongside head. The shogun's concubine slept facing him, while the other two women slept to the left and right, with their backs to the lovers. They were forbidden to either look at the shogun or to fall asleep.

The next morning, the boudoir spies had to make a detailed report from start to finish of the night's events to an elder who waited in an adjacent room. They probably said things like, 'When the shogun said such-and-such, this is what the girl replied.' Or 'The lord, in unusually good spirits, played in such-and-such a way.' If the shogun's bedmate had done anything amiss, she was dismissed from further boudoir service.

The shogun's bed companion, at least at first, must have been acutely aware of the two women lying with their backs to the lovers to the left and right. And in the next room still another woman, called a 'pure person', was on guard, a woman who had to be without prior sexual experience. This, too, must have been a trying duty. The shogun had to perform sexually during the night conscious of three other women alert to every sound that was uttered. Of course, this was the pattern of life, so he probably went about sex as if no one else were present; sometimes, after finishing with the designated concubine, he indulged himself as he pleased with the younger of the two female reporters, the so-called bed supplement. We tend to cherish privacy in sexual relations, but it was denied to the shogun, who had to accept the situation as it was. This kind of surveillance was practised whenever the shogun slept with any woman other than his Number One Wife. The shogun had great power outside the boudoir, but under the bedcovers it was ordained by tradition that he be merely an instrument for the perpetuation of progeny. He had hundreds of harem women at his disposal, but he certainly lacked freedom in the boudoir.

The shogun had to obey still other regulations. For example, after the time of Tokugawa Ieyasu no shogun was allowed in the Great Inner boudoir on the anniversary of the deaths of his predecessors or close relatives. On such days he had to illustrate moral purity and respect for his ancestors through sexual abstinence. There were probably about ten days in a month when the shogun, for one reason or another, could not have sexual relations. Thus the taboos checked any tendency toward sexual license, while affording the shogun periodic opportunities to recoup his sexual powers.

The maidens of the Great Inner were governed by extremely strict rules. They were enclosed in side rooms, where they lived like birds in cages. They were not allowed to leave the harem for the first three years they were there; they could leave for six days at the end of the third year, twelve days during the sixth year, and sixteen days during the ninth year, not, it was decreed, for pleasures of sightseeing or frivolity.

During the fourth shogunate, a new kind of woman arose, one who taught the military arts to women in the harem. Dressed in a rather masculine fashion, she showed the harem occupants how to use swords and spears and how to ride horses. These skills may have been taught to the women in order to provide some outlet for the sexual tension and stress which women confined to the monastic-like existence of the Great Inner inevitably suffered.

As mentioned before, there was an 'under thirty' philosophy about female sex and child-bearing potency, so the harem woman of thirty had to withdraw in emptiness to the women's quarters for the rest of her years. Of course, for many women thirty was the prime of life, an age of heightened interest in amorous play. In her youth, from the middle teens onward, she had to endure the humiliation of having another woman record every idiosyncrasy of her sexual behaviour. She reached full physical maturity, and then, when she had gotten used to the guard system in the shogun's boudoir, the day came when she had to offer a replacement from among her own maids and withdraw from sexual service. She must have felt indescribable anguish.

So the harem women endured an existence marked by ennui and despair, obscure and unloved:

> The women of the harem,
> valued from above
> but in
> enduring harem work,
> overcome by fatigue,
> becoming the mortar,
> again becoming the pestle.*

THE SHOGUN AS LOVERS

The first ruler of the Yedo era, Tokugawa Ieyasu, was the reverse of Hideyoshi† in his choices, for he preferred lower-class to upper-class women. Despite the injunctions against jealousy, he was plagued by jealous wives, and almost all of his fourteen children were borne by concubines. He tried to establish a model for the Tokugawa reign by forbidding young officials to have any communication with his harem ladies.

How did the shoguns who followed Ieyasu fare in the boudoir? Shogun Hidetada of the second generation had such a beautiful Number One wife that he devoted most of his love-making to her and was relatively inactive with subordinate wives. He was reputed to be afraid of his wife. He once made a female bath attendant pregnant, but when his wife discovered this she had the girl expelled from the city.

Iemitsu, the successor to Hidetada, at first was interested only in homosexuality. But he was put in the company of a nun, whom he finally came to desire. When this happened, she was divested of her nun's robes and made a concubine.

*For the original text of this poem, see *Sei no hakubtsu-shi*, p. 67.
†See pp. 43–44.

The fifth-generation shogun was both a scholar and a profligate. His successor Ienobu was said to keep a hundred mistresses, so Ienobu's boudoir life must have been chaotic. He liked to amuse himself in the royal gardens and was a great patron of kabuki players and plays. On occasion he even had plays performed in his bedroom. Present there would be actresses and female impersonators; the impersonators might stay the night in the palace and have sex with the palace maids. Ienobu died young, but before this, in the style of imperial China, he had one of his ministers search the empire for beautiful girls, who then were despatched to his harem.

His successor, Ietsugu, became shogun when a mere five years old, so he was assigned Minister Kambe Akifusa as an 'official protector'. The minister slept in the harem, where he was said to have had relations with more than half of the women. He also appropriated the late Ienobu's beloved concubine. The ill-fated Ietsugu died in childhood, and the man who succeeded him raped a bath attendant, forcing her to wive him.

Ninth-generation Shogun Ieshige, a born woman-hunter, went to such excesses that he died at the early age of seventeen, prostrated by nervous exhaustion. The last two of the Tokugawa shoguns were especially noted for amorous dalliance; the first concentrated his affections on a favoured concubine, and the second had twenty-one concubines in addition to his Number One Wife. In general, we can describe the age of the shoguns as one in which their ministers surrounded them with women to ensure that they would have progeny and perpetuate their lineage.

As mentioned previously, the shogun was the only man with access to the Great Inner Harem. Women there were confined, allowed to leave the premises to visit temples or attend plays only on special occasions. When a shogun died, his concubines were forced to revere his memory in faithful, nunlike solitude. They must have spent lonely lives, especially those who had served as boudoir companions for the night. Some tried to escape this solitary fate; there was the case of a concubine who had an affair with a palace carpenter and was put to death when someone turned informer. Male actors who went in and out of the palace in connection with performing plays there might consort with palace ladies, meeting in one of the more than twenty teahouses bordering a nearby pond. A favoured consort of the sixth-generation shogun was exiled along with all her accomplices when it was discovered that she was secretly having an affair with a merchant. At the beginning he had invited her to see a play.

There were two main categories of women in the harem, those who served the shogun and those who served his principal wife. A wet nurse originated this system during the rule of third-generation Shogun Iemitsu. The harem was divided into Central Inner and Great Inner sections, with a door in between. Theoretically, the shogun was the only man who could enter there. When a concubine reached thirty, she receded to the background, where, if she had borne children, she perhaps wielded some influence in harem politics.

It may have been the restraints imposed by the system of 'fragrant spying' in the shogun's boudoir* that led so many of the shoguns to have intercourse with the female attendants at the baths. This was the one sexual activity in which they could indulge without feeling spied upon. The Japanese followed the Chinese practice of referring to imperial harem occupants as numbering three thousand, though the actual number of females in the Great Inner was probably only about a tenth of this figure. But in addition to the three hundred or so harem women, there were serving girls working there, so many women were involved. Since the shogun had relations with only a fraction of these, the rest must have hungered for love. The main divertissement was viewing plays, which could be attended by women in the harem once every three days.

The shogun bathed once daily in the morning, as did his feudal lords, called *daimyo*. Beautiful attendants brought in hot water, mixing it with cold water to achieve the desired temperature. While this was going on, it was a custom of the *daimyo* to drink wine and revel in the sight of beauty. The shogun entered the baths complete nude, attended by the maids. Generally, whenever men or women of the upper-class entered the baths, they had everything done for them. This included having their garments removed and being bathed, during which time they would not say a word. They were used to being so treated from childhood, so it caused them neither embarrassment nor shame.

CHILDREN OF THE HOT BATHS

In the baths, the shoguns were much freer sexually than in the bedroom since not one reported about them there. They must have frequently been aroused by the touch of female bath attendants, with arousal leading to intercourse. The issue of such encounters

*See pp. 46–47.

were called 'children of the hot baths'. However, even this freedom was finally taken away from the shoguns, for it was contrary to the Tokugawa system of sexual regulation. The eighth shogun Yoshitsune and his successors were not allowed to take hot baths within the Great Inner, as had their predecessors. The Great Inner was not the shogun's private home but rather the dwelling place of his wives and concubines. He normally resided in the Central Inner section, in a masculine world, and it was there that he took his meals. Technically speaking, therefore, there was no need for him to take baths in the women's quarters since he could bathe just as well in the Central Inner. The last three shoguns used the female quarters only for sharing the boudoirs with wives and concubines, allegedly to secure heirs. The shogun was not all-powerful, subject as he was to supervision by his mother and by the elder concillors who were his father's contemporaries.

There were many hot baths for harem residents, differentiated according to rank. There were different baths for the shogun, his wives, his concubines, and the maids. Unlike the masses, the women went into the baths completely nude.

THE DUTY OF WIPING THE MAJESTIC BUTTOCKS

The system of having everything done for a shogun even extended to defecation. In this instance, a servant accompanied him and did everything to ensure that he would not soil his hands. The constant use of incense probably disguised the odour of the faeces somewhat. The psychology of the times was such that to a shogun there was nothing strange about having someone else wipe his buttocks. The female aristocrats of the Great Inner, perched above the masses like lofty clouds, were also said to have had this service performed for them.

SECOND WIVES

The *daimyo*, or feudal lords of Yedo, having to leave their principal wives behind them in the capital, usually took second wives with them on their travels. The second wife almost rivalled the first in influence; she was generally from a good Kyoto family, though women of poor families were also occasionally chosen. The *daimyo* was limited to taking as concubines those women recommended by his first wife. Nevertheless, wives did get jealous of concubines. The *daimyo* installed concubines away from his principal mansion in Yedo, and in this less formal atmosphere he must have been comparatively free, informal, and at ease. He took them to parties and plays. While the wife recommended the concubines, she had no way to check on how they were behaving with her husband in their homes set up apart from the principal residence. There is one famous story about a jealous *daimyo*'s wife who became infuriated when her husband returned to Yedo from a trip and went past her home to that of his concubine. When he later went to see his wife, she said that it was normal for husbands to visit their wives first to ascertain that all was well. But to see the concubine first, she remarked, as he had done, meant he was trying to make a fool of the wife. She spoke to him courageously, showing that the first wife of a *daimyo* could be a wife in fact as well in name, taking seriously the Confucian injunction to admonish the husband when he acted improperly.

HAREMS OF THE DAIMYO

The *daimyo* had harems similar to those of the shogun, but on a much smaller scale. Only women were allowed within. When the *daimyo* took a harem woman to bed, as in the case of the shogun another woman also attended the bedroom to note each sound and utterance. And on reaching the age of thirty, bed partners of the *daimyo* also had to retire. The scale was smaller, but *daimyo* wives also had some influence in appointing or dismissing maids and in determining how they were to be dressed.

YEDO MARRIAGE

Parents of the Yedo era arranged the marriages of their children, but still love attachments arose. Love in such instances was usually called 'un-good', because it constituted a flaunting of the arranged-marriage system. Boys and girls were kept apart from the age of six on, so romantic involvements were usually between servants or between young master and servant – in other words, those living in the same house in close proximity would fall in love. When the 'un-good' was discovered, the transgressors would be personally judged by the master of the house, who could go to the extreme of ordering their decapitation. But there were humane exceptions to the harsh treatment of lovers. The fifth shogunate, for example, mercifully encouraged the householder to assume ignorance of the affair so that the couple might escape through elopement. Further down the social scale, there were also involvements concerning which no questions were asked.

If a wife committed adultery, it was perfectly proper for the husband to decapitate her and her lover on the spot. This right was given not only to the aggrieved samurai but to all city house-holders as well. However, sometimes wives and their lovers escaped; the samurai would assist each other in pursuit, hoping to apprehend and decapitate the fugitives for the sake of their collective honour. It was considered very shameful for the husband to be so cuckolded that he had to set out in pursuit of the lovers. The samurai who indulged in illicit affairs was scorned as being unmanly and dishonourable, but during the eighth shogunate adultery flourished among the samurai, showing that no one was immune to biological forces.

CLASSES OF CONCUBINES

Concubines of the Yedo era usually had only one master, but some of them were shared by three or four men. Their number increased, and by the twelfth shogunate the practice of keeping such women had become widespread among the samurai and the townspeople. There was a class distinction, with the concubines of powerful merchant families much more highly regarded than were those of the lower classes.

SHOPGIRLS

In the Tokugawa era (as in modern India), women did not work in shops where they could be seen by the customers, regardless of the size of the establishment. The rare appearance of even a wife was considered remarkable. The only exceptions were the stores selling sundry goods that were managed by ex-concubines. But women began to work in shops little by little, so that during the ninth shogunate the title 'shopgirl' was coined. In an age of con-cealment of females, the woman who exhibited herself to outsiders was looked down on as disreputable, but there was a demand for her presence.

80

Bathhouses scattered throughout the city of Yedo and just beyond its moats served as social gathering places for the townspeople and afforded relaxation from the daily work routine. The customers would chat with one another about the news of the day and relax in the heated waters. Cheap public bathhouses were first set up early in the Yedo era, the custom being for men to use the baths first, after which women were allowed to enter. But by about 1650 it had become common for men and women to share the use of the baths as well as the bath utensils. Both men and women wore loincloths, but there were many opportunities for naked bodies to touch and for Confucian mores to be breached. In the late eighteenth century, the authorities tried to prohibit mixed bathing by statute, but without much success, and the custom remained in various places until 1885, well into the Meiji eras. The male and female sections were separated by only a slender board placed in the middle of the soaking tub, and it was a simple matter for men to reach the women's section by ducking under the board.

Girls at the hot springs waited on male customers, entertaining them on the second floor after they had emerged from the baths. They plied them with food and drink, sang and danced for them, and engaged in intercourse for a price. These establishments enjoyed a great success until they were completely prohibited in 1657 because they threatened the financial well being of the much more elaborate and expensive Yoshiwara brothels.

WOMEN'S UNDERGARMENTS

Today it is common practice for the Japanese to wear long underwear, but such garments were unknown to women in the Tokugawa age. Japanese women started wearing long underwear during the eleventh shogunate, when the shogun's personal geisha set the fashion. This is reminiscent of imperial China, where the fashion-setters came from the palace and the highest-priced female residents of the gay quarters. In Japan, at first only prostitutes wore long underwear, but in the years that followed it became a general custom. Today almost all Japanese women wear such underwear beneath the kimono. The colour of the underwear was originally pure white, as it was considered embarrassing for it to be noticed by others, but by the end of the fourth shogunate a few women had started to wear coloured stockings and petticoats.

*For more detailed information, including citation of primary sources, see *Higuchi, Kojin sambyaku-gojunen*, pp. 37–43.

These were placed on dolls as well, and the practice spread. In the Yedo era, women of the famed Yoshiwara brothels started wearing coloured undergarments, and got a very favourable reaction from their customers. So the modern Japanese custom of wearing undergarments in various colours had its antecedent in the innovations begun during the Tokugawa era.

A BRIEF HISTORY OF PROSTITUTION IN JAPAN

The earliest known prostitutes in Japan were the shamanesses, described in an earlier chapter, and the nuns. There was a saying to the effect that ' . . . what the monk bought was a nun'. The Buddhists regarded fornication by monks or nuns as one of the five great evils, as serious as killing one's parents or a holy sage. Nevertheless, the nun of antiquity, unlike the contemporary nun, was able to prostitute herself. She was referred to by different names, some of which implied that she was a peripatetic whore who frequented the shrines. A work written in 1690 described how nuns had abandoned all goodness and purity in order to group together, ornately dressed and adorned, and sell themselves. They travelled about looking for male customers, but if conditions were right they might remain in one place. As in ancient Babylonia and Assyria, the history of prostitution in Japan is associated with the shrines and temples which attracted the masses. Nuns gathered in populous shrines in Kyoto, for example, and there brothel districts, such as the Gion quarter, gradually developed.

There were many gradations of prostitute-nuns, including the upper-class songstresses referred to by the novelist Saikaku. A German doctor named Engelbert Kaempfer (1651–1716), who arrived in Nagasaki in 1690, said in his detailed notes that he had encountered singing nuns along the road during two trips from Nagasaki to Yedo. He referred to them as a special religious gathering of young women beggars, who, while called nuns, differed from ordinary Buddhist nuns. They were all beautiful and amiable, noted Kaempfer, and they could be seen on almost any large road in Japan. They waited in groups of twos and threes for upper-class men, and when such men came by they would remain at their sides and entertain them with continuous singing. These comments by Kaempfer indicate he may have failed to realise that the 'singing nuns' he observed were prostitutes. Except for having shaven heads, such nuns looked and behaved like other whores. Some of the prettiest ones had love affairs with samurai. One nun called Haro Taro is remembered by posterity for having fulfilled a love-suicide pact with the son of a rice dealer. In addition to the singing nuns, there were also nun-prostitutes who plied their trade on boats.

KABUKI PLAYERS

Kabuki players tended to be artists by day and prostitutes by night. They performed by day in large groups, wearing bright apparel, and at night they were summoned to feasts, following which they slept with the guests. This is why the shogunate in 1666 strictly forbade kabuki players, restricting this unique form of drama to male performers only, a custom which prevails to the present day.

THE YOSHIWARA QUARTER

During the Tokugawa age, brothels were scattered about the city of Yedo. In 1612 an enterprising brothel manager proposed to the government that it consider the advantages of placing all brothels and houses of assignation in one quarter of the city.* He argued that once the government did this, it would find it easier to uphold social order and public morality. The petition was granted in 1617, and the government assisted in the construction of a series of brothels in one section of the city called Yoshiwara, in the vicinity of Nihonbashi District, completing the project in about ten years. These houses were strictly regulated. Certain rules were to be followed:

1. The brothel owner had to report suspicious characters.
2. The customer could not stay at the house more than twenty-four hours.
3. Prostitutes could not be forced into the trade through kidnapping or other illegal acts.
4. Brothel women could not wear extravagantly expensive clothing.
5. The rooms could not be too lavish.

There were three classes of prostitutes, and, according to one text, in the early period they numbered 75 in Class A, 31 in Class

*For this information and that which follows, see J. E. DeBecker's excellent monograph about the Yoshiwara called *The Nightless City* (Yokohama, Shanghai, Bremen, Max Nossler and Company, third edition, preface dated 1899). See Longstreet, Stephen and Ethel, *Yoshiwara: City of the senses* (McKay, New York, 1970), for a more literary description of the quarter.

B, and 881 in Class C. Prices varied accordingly.

The Class A prostitute was not only the most expensive but a prospective client had to make an appointment with her considerably in advance. Class B and Class C whores might stand in line before a special shop, singing popular songs and playing the banjo-like samisen. They might also smoke tobacco through long cigarette holders or make a forward motion by offering the tiny Japanese pipe called *kiseru* to passers-by. They later appeared in special cages twice a day from noon to 8 p.m. and then again till midnight, when the whorehouse was closed.*

When the quarters at the Yoshiwara were first opened, the samurai class was well monied, but it came to be supplanted in opulence by the merchant class. But the merchants were looked down on as socially inferior to samurai, farmers, and artisans, and they were subject to oppressive treatment by the military. The prostitution quarters afforded them an escape from social constrictions and a place where they could find release from socially imposed frustrations. Their class gradations were not recognised, and they could confront the samurai in a brothel directly and without fear.

In 1656 brothel owners were informed that the houses would have to be moved elsewhere, a move which was expedited when the Yoshiwara was razed by a devastating fire that raged for three days in the spring of 1657. The brothels, reopened in a section called the 'New Yoshiwara', were completed in September, 1657, and the quarters flourished there for three centuries until 1958 when Japan officially outlawed prostitution. The government was determined to have all Yedo prostitutes registered and controlled, and in 1668 it raided unlicensed brothels and forced their 512 occupants into the New Yoshiwara, giving them enough plots of ground on which to build seventy-five small houses there.

BROTHEL PROCEDURES

On arriving at the brothel, the customer first was ushered into a room called a 'transaction parlour'. There he was served tea and tobacco by a young girl. Then another girl brought in cups and dishes, and while this was being done the prostitute he had requested came into the parlour and sat opposite him, somewhat off to one side. The customer handed the cup of tea to the young

*Anonymous, *Notes on the History of the Yoshiwara of Yedo*; Yokohama, *Japan Gazette*, 1894, p. 18.

84

servant, who in turn gave it to the prostitute. She went through
the motions of pretending to partake of it – this was a ritual,
symbolising that she accepted the customer. (Like a sumo wrestling bout, the preliminaries had to be performed in measured,
leisurely, and classically-prescribed ways before the protagonists
could meet in amorous combat.) Then, in response to someone's
informing her that she was being called, the whore went out of the
room and changed her clothes. During this interval, wine was
opened and food brought in. The customer drank the wine with a
geisha, and the sounds of the samisen began to be heard. When
the prostitute returned, she did not speak to the guest or drink
with him, and she rarely glanced at him. No matter how many
wine cups were offered her, she declined and sat looking straight
ahead, enhancing the drama and the mystery of the unknown.
And the more the customer ate and drank, the more interested he
became in his demure but unfathomable hostess. Then finally
someone said, 'Over there,' and a young servant led the customer
to the prostitute's room. At this point, the other women of the
house withdrew. The man was finally united with his prostitute,
and he paid the bills the next morning at the teahouse affiliated
with the brothel.

The second visit was marked first by a congratulatory ceremony
in which the customer expressed his felicitations through the medium of the young servant. This time the prostitute came immediately to the room and talked to the guest. She took several
cups of wine, offering one to the young girl in the form of a
congratulatory toast. This wine, which cost the same as the services of the prostitute, in Japanese feudal times must have signified
that a kind of brothel marriage had been consummated.

From the third visit on, the guest became a familiar customer.
During the third visit, he paid a sum to an old woman in attendance
plus a sum referred to as the 'bed flower', which was about four
times the price of the prostitute's favours, and received the gift of
a purse in exchange. He was then treated with familiarity. The
chopsticks he was to use were decided on, and his name was
written on them:

> He removed the girdle
> which, for three meetings,
> had tantalised his heart and eyes.

Thereafter he could be washed in bed, alongside the woman. When
he left in the morning, someone accompanied him as far as the
main gate. Many of the whores, although they had not spoken to

him at the first meeting, now smiled in his presence. Some were highly skilled in the niceties of the parlour but lacking in sexual technique; others were just the reverse. A prostitite who was pleased by a guest on the first meeting might delight him with one of her poems. Some guests were treated like old customers somewhat earlier than others, from the second meeting on.

THE LIFE OF THE YOSHIWARA PROSTITUTE

The life of the Yoshiwara prostitute was repressive. In all but the finest brothels, the women were usually exhibited in cages, with the class of the house indicated by the height of the bars; the lowest class had horizontal instead of vertical bars. These distinctions were not done away with until 1872, when the status of the prostitute was greatly liberalised.

Almost all of these women were forced into the profession because of dire poverty, ferreted out by a group of professional panderers who went about the country in search of girls in economic straits, procuring, buying, and sometimes even kidnapping them. There were legal efforts to curb this traffic in human misery, but the pimps continued to prosper until the Meiji era, when the Judicial Department on October 7, 1872, issued a law freeing all prostitutes from bondage. The losses sustained by brothel-keepers as a consequence of this official act were said to have been enormous. After that the brothel owners assumed the duties of the pimp, concentrating their recruiting efforts in areas devastated by earthquake, fire, flood, or poor crops. DeBecker cites statistics to prove the success of their efforts, stating that in 1899 fully forty per cent of the 3,000 inmates of the Yoshiwara were from Gifu and Aichi Prefectures, the prefectures which had recently suffered severely from natural disasters. When a district was badly hit by misfortune, concluded DeBecker, 'the various brothel-keepers proceed to the spot in order to see what game they can buy at cheap rates.'

The prostitute was supposed to remain in the brothel until twenty-five years of age, although the average age was twenty-seven. She could regain her freedom in the following ways: the expiration of her contract, the purchase of her contract by her parents, or death. A fourth way, one which most of the women earnestly desired, was redemption by a guest. The guest paid the redemption money and the woman's debts, and with the agreement of her parents the contract was returned to them. She then went to live with her benefactor.

Until she regained her freedom, the prostitute suffered extreme exploitation. In the Yoshiwara, the brothel master would take three-quarters of the proceeds, leaving only one-quarter for the woman. Debts she owed were deducted from her share, so her actual income was even lower. She had to pay for medical treatment, hairdressing, cosmetics and clothes, so it was not easy for her to get by on her own resources. There was virtually no way for her to escape.

ILLNESS IN THE BROTHEL

While the upper-class prostitute who sickened was well treated, with the brothel owner going to considerable expense to cure the illness, the lower-class woman was either sent to a quack doctor or left to suffer in misery in some out-of-the-way room, unnoticed by the other women. Brothel keepers dreaded the thought of a corpse in the rooms. When a whore was at death's door, to avoid the burial expenses the master would summon her parents and return the girl to them, together with her contract of services. If too far from home, she was simply interred in a general burial place nearby:

> In a pauper's coffin
> she is hurried to the grave,
> solitary little maid to mourn her.

In one extreme instance, a prostitute who was ill with a malignant disease spoke to the brothel owner about it, but he told her not to see a doctor but to pray to the God of Fire, Fudosama, for relief. However, the disease got no better. The woman was not allowed to rest and her old customers, feeling sorry for her, brought her patent medicines. But she did not respond to them. She was unable to bear her circumstances any longer, so she fled to the home of a man she knew, but the brothel owner, accompanied by four or five local ruffians, pursued her. They set up a lookout, seized her when she went out at night to the hot baths, and brought her by force back to the brothel in a rickshaw.

She was then shut up and guarded in a room which had glass on three sides, so she could be viewed from the parlour, and was threatened with starvation unless she took in guests.

There were occasional double suicides in the brothel, in which the prostitute went to death with her lover because they could not be joined otherwise owing to the pressure of circumstances.

> Alas!
> Poor maple leaves,
> crushed and scattered
> by the cold wind.

The bodies of these double suicides would first be exposed to public view for three days and then buried like dogs. Their hands and legs were tied together and the corpses were wrapped in straw matting and thrown into a common grave, the whorehouse owners believing that burial in this fashion would prevent their being haunted by vengeful ghosts.

The whorehouse compound at Yoshiwara was apart from the shrine, separated by a series of rice-fields. Only one road led to its main gate, so it was like an island into itself, a fortress of flesh to which its inmates were confined while a spark of beauty remained. The whores adopted a special vocabulary and way of speech, thereby disguising social origins. To say 'there is', for example, they used *arinsu* instead of the usual *arimasu*, and the quarter was even referred to as if it were a foreign country, the 'Country of Arinsu' (Arinsu Koku). Many individual studies of the Yoshiwara were made by its decades of male admirers, and while the titles of most of these works are a matter of record, usually they are either no longer extant or virtually inaccessible.

Yearly lists were kept in the nineteenth century of the women in each of the houses, with the best ones specifically designated and a price list appended. Included in these listings were male and female geisha. Prospective customers must have thus had fairly easy recourse to a guide-book on whores of the 'five dollars a day' (and up!) variety.

Today nothing remains, except a marker showing the approximate location of the great gate through which one entered, and a shrine to the quarter's victims of the 1923 earthquake and the World War II fire bombings. In one site even the graves of prominent courtesans have been done away with. In the modern hustle and bustle of the Asakusa section of Tokyo, that three-centuries old institution we refer to as Yoshiwara's 'nightless city' seems but a figment of the imagination. As one stone marker at a shrine plaintively notes, when the anti-prostitution law was enforced on April 1, 1958, the work of centuries vanished in a single night.*

The brothel quarters in the renowned Shinjuku section of Yedo, built at the start of the Tokugawa era, were demolished for a time but rebuilt in about 1764. Women of the inns worked as prostitutes at Shinagawa, Shinjuku, Itabashi and Senju in Yedo and they were tacitly recognised. There were also lower-class prostitutes and publicly authorised ones. Provincial women provided services to travellers at each relay station. There were three quarters comparable to the Yoshiwara, the Shimabara and Gion quarters in Kyoto and the Shinmachi quarter in Osaka. The highest class of Kyoto courtesan exerted influence till the end of the Tokugawa era: she was the first of four gradations of desirability and by far the most costly.

LIVING, THE BITTER SEA;
DEAD, THE TEMPLE PURE SECLUDED.

The temple Pure Secluded ('Jokanji' in Japanese) still flourishes today in Tokyo's Minami Senju District, immune for the past three centuries from the earthquake and fires that have ravaged its neighbours. Here is where 25,000 Yoshiwara whores were interred at death, tossed indiscriminately into large man-made holes created within the temple grounds. This was the practice from 1657 to the first quarter of the 20th century, but after that time the skeletal bones were dug up and placed in buried urns. For many of the whores life must have been a 'bitter sea', but they were subject to further humiliations when they died. The corpse was stripped naked, deprived of even hair ornaments, wrapped in a straw matting, and thrown into one of the holes. (Hence, the other name by which the temple was known, *Nagekomi-dera*, meaning the 'being thrown-into temple'.) The dead whore was handled like an animal, perhaps owing to a superstition that by treating her this way the living could prevent her spirit from returning to earth to wreak its vengeance. The temple still has on hand the records that it kept of each whore's death date, religious name, first name, and the whorehouse to which she belonged.

*The writer toured the area on July 16, 1970, vainly trying to uncover evidence of the past. *Toruko* bath-houses are now a conspicuous sight, located where the whorehouses used to be.

Yoshiwara is the butterfly,
Shinjuku the dance of the horse-fly.

In the horse manure
of Yotsuya and Shinjuku
beautifully blossom
the iris flowers.

The Yoshiwara catered to a more refined clientèle than did the whorehouse quarters at Shinjuku, established in 1772. These flourished till 1958, when the law was enforced which made prostitution illegal. Today the area is known for its bathhouses, bars, theatres, and 'nude studios'. (The studios feature nudes who adopt a variety of poses, with no musical accompaniment and no stripping.) The section there called kabuki-cho ('the street of kabuki'), now frequented by hippies, was located in the heart of the prostitution area, featuring illicit sex at reduced prices. The most famous whore there, Shirato, had her deeds commemorated in a mid-nineteenth century *kabuki* play.

There was little understanding of sanitation and of communicable diseases, and syphilis became commonplace, with almost all of the lower-class prostitutes ravaged by it. When they died, many of them would be interred at the Burial Grounds of No Affinity. After contracting syphilis, there was an interval in which the patient seemed to revert to normal, and in Tokugawa Japan the price for such a syphilitic woman was higher than that for one who had no illness at all, perhaps because the assumption was made that she had been cured and was therefore immune to further disease.

It was not until 1867, or well into the Meiji era, that a hospital, the first of its kind in Japan, was established in Yokohama to treat prostitutes who were venereally diseased. It came into official existence largely through the efforts of an English physician named Newton, and subsequently physical examinations were made twice monthly in six of the main brothel quarters. The results showed that the infection rate at about the turn of the century was a little over 6 per cent and that each woman received on the average 445 to 460 guests yearly.*

THE MODERN RED-LIGHT DISTRICT AT SHINJUKU

Shinjuku is a bustling, prosperous section of Tokyo to the present day, on a par with the Ginza, but it achieved fame many decades

*DeBecker.

ago through its 'streets of joy'. These flourished till April 1, 1958, when the law outlawing prostitution was first enforced (two years after its enactment). Till that time Shinjuku contained both licensed red-light and unlicensed green-light districts, in which prostitution flourished. The red-light district, being located in the section called Shinjuku-nichome, was usually referred to simply as *nichome*. Besides this red-light district, Tokyo then had many others in the sections called Yoshiwara, Shinagawa, Suzuki, Tamo-no-i and others, but Shinjuku became prominent because it did such a thriving business. Its green-light district, called either Hanazono or Kabukicho, was cheaper than *nichome*. It was therefore patronised primarily by young students and modest wage-earners.

My Japanese friend and informant, who naturally wishes to remain anonymous, tells me that he first visited *nichome* in the summer of 1954, just when he was getting ready to enter the university. It then had from sixty to seventy houses which were legally required to refer to themselves euphoniously as 'special eating and drinking houses'. Each house had from five to ten women in it. As night came on, they would apply powder and rouge, stand by the entrance to the houses or by the windows facing the street, and call out to passers-by to come inside. But they were forbidden by law to latch on to prospective customers outside on the streets. The men would carefully look over the 'merchandise' and, if one of the women made an attractive impression, stroll over the entrance and talk about prices. There were three kinds of arrangements, for which the price range from 1954 to 1957 was generally as follows:

Short time:	$1.50 to $2.00	
Time:	$2.00 to $3.00	
All night:	(from dusk onwards)	$9.00 to $11.00
All night:	(after midnight)	$6.00 to $9.00

'Short time' meant one emission only, 'time' implied a fifty minute interval, during which some men might be able to have two emissions, while 'all night' was self-explanatory. The all night customer might enter the hot baths with his chosen whore, go out to dinner with her, and go about things in a much more leisurely fashion.

In the green-light district of Shinjuku, one didn't enter the house until the price question was satisfactorily resolved. But at *nichome's* red-light district, it was customary for each house to have a bar on the first floor and rooms on the second and third floors. Nobody actually came there to drink, but the houses had to have the bar set-up in order to get a license to operate. The girls furnished their rooms as they pleased, installing their own furniture, and sometimes they served tea in their rooms to customers who had paid for fifty minutes or more. The bedding was of course always in a state of readiness. When the customer went to the girl's room, he first handed over the sum as agreed upon. Then he took off his clothes and had intercourse, usually using a condom. Women who worked as whores got their sex educations from the house madams and generally became very adept sex partners. Even if they didn't feel anything, they would cry out and put on a big act to excite the man and get him to ejaculate more quickly. After it was all over, the woman cleansed herself and the man; in some houses, V.D. preventive medicine was placed in the toilet and there the girl would treat the man's privates.

Women working in the *nichome* red-light district were medically inspected twice weekly at Shinjuku Hospital, on Tuesdays and Fridays. Anyone discovered to be diseased was ordered by her doctor to stay at the hospital until she was completely cured. (Of course, it's impossible to say categorically that this was strictly observed.) But on Tuesday and Friday nights customers would arrive at the houses early and in greater numbers than usual, in the belief that girls allowed to work on those days were free of disease.

The history of *nichome* can't be compared with that of a much older district like Yoshiwara, but there as well some old customs and sayings were preserved. One's first visit was referred to as a *shokai* or 'first meeting', while the second visit to the same girl was called *ura* or 'reverse side', probably implying that the man returned the obligation he had incurred at the first meeting. With the third visit, he became a *najimi* or 'regular customer'. The second visit was considered morally obligatory, whether he liked the girl or not. Once a man had selected a girl from a house, he had to stay with her as long as he patronised that house; this was another of the unwritten laws.

The girls who worked in the red-light and green-light districts of Tokyo were largely from poor peasant families of northeast origin. Commerce in human beings was legally outlawed about a century ago in Japan, but nevertheless many girls were forced into whoredom in order to absolve their parents of heavy debts. Then there were girls who, having left home to seek career and fortune in the big cities, fell into the clutches of gangsters and pimps. Most of the girls were young, sixteen or seventeen, lying about their ages and claiming to be the legal adult age of twenty when they were really only in their mid-teens. In about 1955 a case was publicised in which police arrested a house operator for employing minors under seventeen years of age, but teenage whores were a common sight.

BATH-HOUSE GIRLS

With the public establishment of the brothels, private prostitution was banned, but bath-house girls were tolerated officially. As the ban became stricter (as in modern postwar Japan!), the number of bath-house girls increased, to such a degree that the Yoshiwara declined in popularity. In the late sixteenth and seventeenth centuries, young women worked in cheap public bath establishments, cleansing the guests and dressing their hair. Like the kabuki players, they were bath-house attendants by day and prostitutes by night. Feasts were held each night on the second floor of the establishment, where the girls, wearing party dresses, poured drinks, sang, and beguiled the guests. A large bath-house in the Kanda section of Yedo, famed for its beautiful attendants, was even frequented by renowned samurai. The baths were very popular, being cheaper in price and easier to enjoy than the much more formal Yoshiwara quarters. So many customers frequented the baths that the Yoshiwara was threatened financially. Influential and monied people of the quarter put pressure on the authorities, and in 1627 bath-houses were forbidden to employ more than three women. But even then business flourished, so finally in 1656 more than two hundred houses were closed. Almost all of the bath-house owners thus affected then opened brothels at the Yoshiwara. This was the exact reverse of what was to happen three centuries later, when in 1958 prostitution was outlawed and the Yoshiwara quarter lost its brothels but gained a new row of Turkish baths in their place.

GEISHA

The term 'geisha' was first used at the Yoshiwara, to distinguish the women who sold their arts to men but not their flesh. But even the geisha went the way of prostitution eventually, and the number of whores increased. By 1798 there were no more geisha to be seen in Yedo, but a few years later they made a strong comeback around the Fukagawa section. And their popularity increased. Men who preferred that which was elegant but non-ostentatious frequented the geisha, who was made up in a subtler and less obvious fashion than the usual prostitute. At first, geisha were not allowed to work in the brothel quarters, but in 1848 an order was promulgated to the effect that there could be one geisha assigned to each house. This order was misconstrued, with the result that several geisha, rather than only one, came to be so employed. Some of the Fukagawa geisha, known for their artistry, were proud that they did not sell their flesh, but most were in essence private prostitutes. When customers entered their rooms, they could not help noticing that the bedding had been spread.

OTHER KINDS OF NIGHT FLOWERS

Some women in this era set up small huts to be used only at night, perhaps a precursor of the nocturnal food-and-drink shacks still to be seen along the approaches to Yokohama's former brothel area. However, in Tokugawa times prostitutes spread straw mats in the huts and beckoned to prospective customers. During the day the huts were usually torn down. These 'prostitutes of the huts' ranged in age from fifteen or sixteen to about forty. Also among them were many aged and sickly women, no longer employable in the brothel quarters. The thin ones dressed like young girls; the very old ones dyed their white hair black and bound the hair in a *shimada* coiffure associated with youth – the intent was deception, the goal livelihood. Women who had lost their noses through the ravages of disease made false noses out of candles and camouflaged their scars with powder. These were prostitutes of the lowest class imaginable.

BEAN JAM DUMPLINGS OF THE BOATS

Among the many different gradations of prostitutes in the Tokugawa era were the lowly 'bean jam dumplings of the boats'. The bean jam dumplings was a simile for the Yedo women who ostensibly sold dumplings at the river's edge but in actuality were selling their flesh to sailors, travellers, and whoever else they could entice or drag to their sides. There were several explanations as to why such women were referred to as 'bean jam dumplings'; one writer alleged that this was a secret word for the vagina, based on the resemblance of the steamed dumpling to the vagina. Women also

94

referred to such dumplings as *oman*, which was said to have a pronunciation close to that of a slang word for the vagina. Either of these explanations would associate the term with vulgar words connoting sexual intercourse and its paid practitioners. Still another writer claimed that the word for dumpling came into use when riverbank prostitutes began to ply their trade under the pretext of selling dumplings. It was also stated that in the mid-seventeenth century a certain dumpling seller became so intimate with prostitutes around the Fukugawa river district that he let them use his commercial slogan, which became a simile for riverbank prostitution.

Boatside prostitutes in Japan had a long history, being cited as far back as the seventh-eighth century anthology of poems called the *Manyoshu*. In the mid-Heian era there must have been many such women along the banks of Osaka Bay and the Yodozawa district, the latter area incidentally being a traditional centre for profligation until modern times. The Yedo variety was often cheap, worn out, and ravaged by venereal disease:

> Nose falling off,
> crying voice,
> concealing her fallen body.
> Below the bean jam dumpling,
> pulling out his lowly string of cash.
> Bean paste pleasures of the fields,
> cold-cool wine;
> the small boat at midnight,
> the drunken guest.

This famous poem describes the cheap, syphilitic prostitute of the rivers, calling out to customers from her rush-thatched boat as long as there is a spark of life in her withered frame. These women would go from boat to shore in search of customers, wandering from one abode to the next, relatively immune from official action.

The authorities partially got rid of the river prostitutes in the eighteenth century, but by the end of the shogunate they had made a strong comeback and were much in evidence in Yedo along the canals and on the Sumida River. They were like another low class of whore referred to as a 'nighthawk', though perhaps better dressed and made up. In fact, there were some beautiful women in this group, who sometimes charged four times as much for their favours as did the 'nighthawks'.

Some of the 'dumplings' were so diseased that they could no longer walk; they confined their activities to the boat, not going ashore. The charges varied from about a hundred copper coins for the best in this class to twenty-four coins for the worst.

The scholar to whom we are indebted for this information recollects how in his childhood (after the turn of the century) when a ship stopped in port it would be surrounded by local prostitutes in small boats. The captain would call out to his guests, 'Does anyone need a woman?' The next morning small boats would return to take the prostitutes back to the shore. These women, at the bottom of their social class, must have been a tough breed of flesh sellers, struggling for survival. The drunken guest would soon be relieved of his excess cash; however, we do have one Confucian-oriented tale about how virtue wins out even in the lowliest of places. Almost two hundred years ago, a merchant's clerk was delayed on his way back to Yedo by one of the boat prostitutes, and when he returned to shore he discovered the loss of his master's purse. Horrified, he rowed a boat along the river for seven days and nights, searching for the woman who had led him astray. Finally he found her, and, without reproach, simply informed her that unless he got the purse back he would have to kill himself in order to requite his unpardonable behaviour towards his master. The prostitute relented, silently returning the purse, and on being informed of the incident the master purchased her freedom and arranged for her and the clerk to marry and live together as man and wife.

TEAHOUSE GIRLS

There were no food-and-saké houses in Yedo until the end of the seventeenth century, when one restaurant opened in the Asakusa area and became very popular. Then more restaurants sprang up, though in some of them the women who served the wine were prostitutes. Teahouses along the waterfront also featured pretty girls, perhaps in competition, like the beautiful waitresses seen today in certain Tokyo coffee shops. Such teahouses were pleasing to the eyes of Yedo men, and they were extremely well patronised. This was a time when decent women generally concealed themselves from masculine view, when even merchants would not allow their wives or daughters to work in their shops. The old custom of concealing women from public view explains why the new teahouse waitresses became such objects of attention.

96

WARRIORS AND PROSTITUTES

Towards the end of the shogunate, warriors whose lives were in jeopardy naturally sought comfort from prostitutes. The relevant saying was '. . . at night in the arms of shapely beauties, to grasp on awakening the power of the universe'. Some geisha and upper-class whores became the wives of prominent government ministers; others started as very young concubines of the samurai and became Number One Wives at the death of the wife. About 1868, nightly dance parties were held at a place called Deer's Cry Mansion (*Rokumeikan*), which got its name from a partial reference to banqueting in a Chinese classic called 'The Book of Odes'. The mansion was started in 1881 and completed two years afterwards. Located near modern Hibiya Park, the lavish European-style building was used for diplomatic receptions and parties involving Japanese and foreign statesmen and their wives. Here it was that Japanese women adopted Western-style dress, initiating fashions that eventually spread throughout Japan. The building stood until 1945, when it was burned to the ground during a bombing raid.

The geisha of this era were easily available boudoir companions who would loosen the strings of their girdles as the guests desired and sell their bodies without even bothering to notice who the buyer was. Social change meant loss of stature and position for the military, many of whom had to sell daughters into prostitution in order to survive. This was in contrast to the newly powerful men of the age, the political masters who in their arrogance could summon a geisha to appear before them completely nude. They would then make these geisha the stakes in gambling events. Even if they tried to resist being disrobed, there was no way out -- in a figurative sense, the flesh of such women was trampled upon.

THE NEW MEIJI WOMAN

Early in the Meiji era, one woman argued for the right of her sex to participate in government, and in 1892 and 1893 a group of women writers argued for love and free choice in marriage. The movement towards feminine emancipation received much impetus from the new currents of thinking entering Japan from Europe and America. In 1911, four progressive ladies published an influential journal which advocated female equality. These emancipators even went into the Yoshiwara in an effort to buy out the prostitutes within it.

THE SLAVE INCIDENT

In 1872, a Peruvian cargo ship, carrying about 250 slaves purchased in China, landed in Yokohama. Japan made a worldwide appeal on behalf of the slaves, calling this 'a problem of humanity', and it gained a reputation in many countries as a righteous nation. But the Peruvians rebuked the Japanese in these words: 'It speaks thus, but at present within Japan there are geisha and prostitutes everywhere being bought and sold. Isn't it strange then for them, who have this custom, to criticise the buying and selling of foreign slaves?' There was not the slightest word of rebuttal from the Japanese.

This national embarrassment prompted the Japanese government to action, and in October, 1872 a law was issued which freed the prostitutes. Theoretically, that might have signified the end of the brothel quarters, but the prostitutes were passive and the mood of the times permissive. The brothels were allowed to reopen, with the proviso that women who had left them could return, but of their own volition. The situation eventually reverted to what it had been before the promulgation of the law.

THE ERA OF THE MODERN WOMAN

The Taiso and Showa eras (1912 onwards) were characterised by a diffusion of the doctrine of romantic love throughout Japan. The love affairs of famous stage personalities and other well-known people made the news, effecting slight inroads on the time-hallowed custom of arranged marriages. Women gradually moved forward to take up previously all-male occupations, and there was a sharp increase in the number of bus girls, typists, office workers, and mannequins. The so-called era of the modern woman had arrived. Early in the Showa era 'modern girls' and 'modern boys' began to appear in dance halls and coffee shops holding hands and displaying affection. (This would have been unthinkable in Tokugawa Japan.) In Tokyo, bars sprang up along the Ginza, uniformed waitresses served beer, and fashionable call girls arose. Because these girls clung to men like they were walking sticks, they came to be called 'stick girls'. They got their start as licensed tour guides. Dozens of beautiful girls were recruited for Asakusa coffee houses, and they attracted the patronage of the romance-minded male. Coffee houses and serving maids became commonplace, until there were about fifteen thousand such women in the Ginza district alone.

— TO WEAR OR NOT TO WEAR WESTERN-STYLE PANTIES —

During this period, Western dress styles for women became more popular, though the very Japanese kimono still prevailed. As described in an earlier chapter, late in the Tokugawa period a few women began to wear underpants. However, this was on a very limited scale. As late as the nineteen thirties, the prevailing type of underwear worn by women was a kind of long undershirt which reached to the ankles. A few of the more venturous and Western-oriented ladies adopted underpants, but the feeling was widespread that wearing such panties irritated the private parts. The real inducement to wearing panties occurred in the aftermath of two Tokyo disasters, the earthquake of 1923 and the Shirokiya Department Store fire of December 16, 1932. Female earthquake victims who ran about in their long undershirts were reputedly so embarrassed to be seen in this ugly pose that a clamour for the wearing of Western-style drawers began to be heard. When fire broke out in 1932 at the Shirokiya Department Store, located in a commercial centre of Tokyo, many of the saleswomen fled to the upper floors and finally escaped to the roof. There three of them went to their deaths, preferring not to jump into the rescue nets and trying instead to wrap their kimonos tightly around them to prevent public exposure to the curious gaze of the crowd looking up from the street below. In a real but tragic sense, therefore, they were 'embarrassed to death' by their concern with the traditional proprieties. These deaths were publicised, leading to a slogan calling for everyone to wear Western-style drawers. Women who went mountain-climbing became tragically involved in similar incidents. They would start to ascend a mountain as one human link in a long chain, but if a strong wind blew would instantly grab their skirts to prevent exposure, let go of the cahin, and plunge to their deaths. In 1932, it has been estimated that only one per cent of Japanese women wore underpants; it took another decade for feminine wearing of underpants to become the general rule. With the outbreak of World War II, women had to go to work alongside men and adopt Western dress, which at times included pants and a baggy type of wartime trouser called monpe. Two years after the war ended, the 'Christian Dior look' in lingerie was publicised, influencing Japanese women, and a movement in favour of greater femininity in undergarments gathered momentum. There was also a post-war enthusiasm for wearing panties in a variety of colours, in fact even a different coloured panty or petticoat for each day of the week. (These were referred to as 'weekly panties' or as 'petticoats in seven colours'.)

INTERNATIONAL TRAFFIC IN JAPANESE PROSTITUTES

In 1930, the League of Nations conducted a formal inquiry into international traffic in Asian prostitutes and published the findings two years later. These indicated that the Chinese supplied the largest number of whores moving from one country to another in the late twenties, followed by the Japanese. 'Japanese' was so interpreted as to include Koreans and Formosans, since they inhabited what was then part of the Japanese Empire. Asian prostitutes other than Chinese and Japanese were in much smaller numbers and of much less importance.

Japanese whores flocked to Hong Kong and Singapore before 1920, but the Japanese government came to regard their presence there as a negative factor which obstructed efforts to develop sound overseas interests. It therefore worked through its consular officials and elicited the cooperation of the local authorities in a determined effort to repatriate these women, with such success that more than nine-tenths of the Japanese prostitutes in Singapore- for example, returned to Japan within three years after the policy was initiated. (Local authorities would be asked to refuse to issue licenses allowing Japanese women to practise prostitution.)

In general, the supply of Japanese prostitutes overseas met an almost exclusive demand on their services by Japanese men, who objected strongly to having these women cater to the sexual needs of men from other races. Both the Chinese and Japanese regarded the prostitute among them who associated with men of other nationalities as despicable and the lowest of her class. There was also a strong overseas Japanese demand for geisha, giving added significance to the comment that the Japanese 'on foreign soil tend to reproduce in miniature the social life of their mother country'. Places in China under Japanese municipal administration regulated prostitution in the same way they had regulated it in Japan.

Japanese prostitutes overseas usually joined the profession to get financial relief for their families, incurring a debt with the brothel owner. Japanese government regulations set forth the rate of interest and the proportion of the prostitute's earnings that could be legally retained for repayment of the loan. In 1930, there were 1,408 licensed Japanese prostitutes in the Kwaytung Leased Territory and the South Manchurian Railway Zone. Almost half of these women had no previous occupation – about a fourth were from the farms, close to a tenth were former waitresses, and there were smaller numbers of ex-factory girls, ex-geisha, nurses, fishermen, and housewives. There were almost two thousand geisha in China, three-fourths of whom had had no earlier fixed occupation. These girls were designated for whoredom by their parents at a very early age, with the parents receiving money in advance for the contracts of service. Regulations in Japan and Formosa stipulated that girls under the age of twelve not be employed as geisha. Geisha were sometimes forced to become prostitutes through the coercion of geisha house owners.

The recruitment of Japanese prostitutes in China and elsewhere in the Japanese Empire was accomplished through special employment agencies, set up in accord with Japanese regulations. In such cases the procurer conducted a legitimate business, involved exclusively with Japanese interests and subject to local and central official regulations.

PUBLIC MORALITY

The coffeehouses which flourished between 1915 and 1935 had lights of red, green, and other bright colours in order to convey a Western-associated romantic mood. They would circulate advertisements stressing the allure of their female employees, even though such publication was not immune from official indictment. Stories were written about coffeehouse girls who prostituted themselves to supplement inadequate earnings. More than twenty such coffeehouses were officially closed because of charges of immorality, indicating a loosening of public morality in the big cities.

There was a like tendency for certain restaurants and dressmaking establishments to become offices for prostitute transactions. Many widows and single people patronised dance halls for the purpose of finding love partners, as they still do today, and go-betweens were used to arrange concubinage and prostitution as well as marriage. Female office workers and nurses inveigled into prostitution by unscrupulous go-betweens could be had nightly for a modest fee, while for a larger sum girls of good families were similarly available. The police finally took action, ordering the closing of six go-between offices located in the Asakusa and Aoyama sections of Tokyo.

Thus it was that, with public morality visibly worsening, Japan plunged into the second world war.

XII. Sex and Godliness

Before the advent of Buddhist precepts and Confucian morality, there was frank and clear praise of sex in Japanese poetry and prose. The ancient Japanese sang freely of sex and spoke of it uninhibitedly wherever they happened to assemble. Sex was regarded as a kind of wondrous power, symbolised by the phallus, and phallic worship prevailed from earliest times. This view of sex was sharply opposed by the later moralists, who regarded it as something to be hidden and suppressed. The comment was made that since sex was like a tiger, one should be very careful in nourishing it so as not to be eaten by it. Other moralists condemned sexual behaviour as fit for beasts alone. From sex to faith, from prostitute to nun: In a work by the novelist Saikaku, an old woman who has known thousands of men in her lifetime finally seeks faith and forgiveness. Before the Bodhisattvas she enumerates her lovers and senses the enormity of her wrongdoing. In China, too, the nunnery provided a sanctuary for the repentant prostitute and the woman rejected by the fickleness of fate. A famous example of lover-to-nun was the Heian authoress Sei Shonagon, who had brief love affairs with members of the court and was favoured by the emperor's consort. But when the consort died, leaving Sei Shonagon like a bird on a withered branch, she eventually became a nun. Many graves claim her remains, but no one knows for certain where she wandered or where she was buried. There are stories about her with crude sexual overtones. One says that she cut out her own vagina and threw it into the sea, another alleges that she was killed by a local people who cut out her vagina and threw it into the sea, where it became a shellfish. Here we see the association of vagina and shellfish (including clam, corbicula, and ark shell), for all are Japanese euphemisms for the vagina. Before World War II, there was a famous product of Lake Biwa, a fresh-water clam, to which seasoning was added. It was then dried out, put into a paper bag, and sold. The bag in which it was sold was called 'the maiden of Lake Biwa'.

To the Japansee, mushrooms of the mountains looked like penises and seashells resembled vaginas. The edible mushroom called *matsutake* was thought closest in form to the penis, while among the shellfish the sea mussel was regarded as most like the vagina. This sea mussel was given other names such as 'hair shell' and 'maiden shell'. Since the sea mussel was associated with the vagina, the hairs that grew on it were thought of as the hairs of a woman's sex organ. In many places it was prized as 'the shell which resembles', with an early eighteenth-century reference explicitly stating that the sea mussel was known as 'the lady of the Eastern seas' because of its form. The sea mussel was said to have arisen from the vagina of Sei Shonagon after it was borne out to sea. In some villages, Sei Shonagon, revered as the God of Lower (Body) Ailments, is prayed to on the tenth day of the month.

THE GOD CALLED 'DOKYO'

Dokyo is worshipped because of his great penis, and in an early seventeenth-century work on unusual characteristics he is cited under reference to 'the thickest'. His penis is also likened to the jutting forth of a 'third knee', and in a satirical poem it is compared to the penis of a horse. It's claimed that he wasn't born that way but rather developed his horse-like penis in middle age. He supposedly achieved prominence through becoming the beloved of an empress dowager who lived in the latter half of the eighth century. Folklore was circulated to the effect that when the dowager sickened, Dokyo was one of the priest-doctors summoned to her bedside. She had such a wide vagina that no man could satisfy her, and a search for men with huge penises ensued. Dokyo alone fulfilled her fondest expectations, and in this way he effected an immediate cure. From 765 on, he and the empress dowager shared the bedcovers, an event commemorated through a popular festival. Dokyo, enjoying great political power, was entitled 'King of the Dharma'. He could do anything he wanted; many others in his clan prospered as a consequence, thus showing the awesome power of a mighty penis. It was said that he gave the empress dowager a model of his penis as a masturbational instrument, but when she used it it broke inside the vagina and she could never remove it. The empress died in 770, aged fifty-three, and with her death Dokyo was ousted from power. He returned home and on the way back allegedly cut off his penis, the source of his prosperity and decline. He vanished, but the penis he had left behind was worshipped as God of the Golden (Semen) Essence. And even today there is a mountain peak called The Peak of the Golden Essence.

Not only the penis but its counterpart, the vagina, was also prayed to in the belief that all living things issued from the gate of the living goddess. There were such place names, therefore, as 'Hole Village', referred to in the Ainu language as a 'place of vagina exhibition'. This was sanctified as an area where a goddess had once revealed her vagina. In like fashion, prayers were offered up to holes in caves and alongside lakes. The eighth-century *Kojiki* ('Chronicle of Ancient Events') informs us that when a goddess was killed, wheat and beans sprang forth from her vagina. These were offered to a god, who was delighted with the gift. There is evidence here of an ancient belief in the fecundity of the female sex alone, independent of the male. Thus the sun goddess Ameterasu gave birth to four gods by her own efforts. In the primitive age of random selection, when a child was born the villagers might not be sure of who the father was, and they did not try to find out. They minimised the function of fatherhood, which came to be exalted when the matriarchal society crumbled. Life and production came to centre about the father, who had to have sons to bequeath his assets to them. The woman who desired a child might enter a sea or ocean, to be awaited there by a goddess who inserted the 'golden essence' into her womb, causing her to conceive. Here the male's only role was said to be the widening of the passage to facilitate entrance of the golden essence.

THE TEETH OF THE VAGINA

Japan has its share of these castration-fear stories, which are international in scope and significance.* There is a story in Japan about a bride and groom, who prior to the wedding night, were disturbed by someone who told the bride that the groom's penis was as huge as Dokyo's and the groom that the bride's vagina had teeth in it. On the wedding night the inexperienced couple each

*Cf. the detailed analysis by G. Legman in *Rationale of the Dirty Joke.*

half believed what they'd heard. The groom was afraid of being bitten, so he used his knee instead of his penis, whereupon the bride thought, 'My God! It *is* like Dokyo's,' and she fled from the marriage bed, never to return. There are many stories in Japan about teeth-cutting vaginas, including one about a woman who used her vagina to cut off the penises of nine men as casually as if she were peeling bananas. There is a Taiwanese story with similar implications about a beauty who married a handsome and courageous groom. But he died the morning after the wedding night. The parents then chose another youthful groom for her, but the same thing happened. After many such tragic occurrences, the parents inspected the corpse of one of the grooms and noticed that the penis had been cut off at the root. Then, when they looked at their daughter's vagina, they discovered it had teeth as sharp as a razor's edge. They talked to her about it and then smoothed down the teeth on a grindstone. She then became capable of a happy marriage without a calamitous aftermath for the groom.

There was a god with a black bronze penis called 'Kanamara', prayed to by males who wished to increase their virile powers. He figured prominently in another story about a woman with teeth in her vagina who emasculated a series of grooms on the wedding night. Finally a hero appeared who asked for her hand in marriage. He made a penis of black bronze like that of Kanamara, used it in the bedroom, and broke the vaginal teeth to bits on it. After that, his bride became harmless and a non-castrator. Kanamara was also revered for the removal of evil, the curing of all lower body ailments, and the severing of relations with a concubine. His shrine was cluttered with countless phallic forms, ranging in size from a few inches to several feet and varying in materials from wood to pottery. People around the shrine told one Japanese researcher that Kanamara was inclined to give supernatural assistance to merchants, farmers, barren women, people suffering from venereal diseases, and men with weak penises and women with weak vaginas. He was also worshipped by prostitutes. The believers thus offered phalluses to Kanamara in gratitude for his efficaciousness. Some Japanese still believe in this god and erect shrines to him in Iwate and elsewhere. But believers say that disaster befalls mankind when his supernatural assistance proves to be excessive and cite an instance where village girls were raped, one after the other.

105

There are phallic references in a late Heian song collection, showing that phallic worship in Japan can be traced back more than a thousand years. The Japanese prayed to phallus-shaped stones found along the road, spreading stories of how the worshippers of certain stones became immensely wealthy. The worship of these stones was practised extensively in brothel districts, until the Meiji restoration (last third of the nineteenth century). Wine was offered to Eros-in-stone every morning, after which prayer followed. Many of the suppliants were prostitutes and river merchants.

Phallic objects were sold in shops lining the streets leading to the Kannon ('Goddess of Mercy') statue at Asakusa, ranging in size from six-foot flesh-coloured phalluses to small inch-long playthings. There were the masturbational phallic representations called *harigata*, which, though used by women, were not bought publicly by them. Men bought them instead and gave them to women as presents. A priest lectured in front of the temple to Kannon, illustrating his remarks with wooden phalluses. The temple was near the Yoshiwara prostitution quarters, symbolising the connection between religion and sex in Japan. The priest would gather a crowd together, calling the penis the foremost master of all time and speaking in crude detail of boudoir matters. Phallic objects were also sold openly in the Kansai area at an Osaka temple and, while the scale of buying was smaller than that at Asakusa, there was little inhibition among the purchasers. Women of the Kansai area would buy phalluses as they might fruit and toys, mixing them in with their other purchases. The opening of Japan to the West dealt an official blow to phallic worship, for in March, 1872, prayers to phallic gods were prohibited on the grounds that such observances were offensive to public morality. Officials who found people worshipping phallic objects expropriated such objects and threw them into the river. So many were said to have been thrown into the Sumida River, for example, as to form an imposing sight. Despite the prohibition, until the first decade of the twentieth century phallic representations continued to be sold secretly in specialised shops to geisha and others until a special commercial group was formed to eliminate this trade.

In pre-Meiji Japan there was widespread belief in the benevolent or malevolent properties of animals and insects, and medical prescriptions often consisted of insects placed in red bags. Animals with special properties included eels, lizards, and badgers, while certain insects were considered protection against illness and natural disasters. The weirdest and most frightening of the insects was a kind of tapeworm believed to repose in the womb. Another worm climbed on the head and made the hair white; still another got into the stomach and harmed the five internal organs. A lower variety, one lodged in the feet, was injurious to tranquility and sexual potency. In other words, tapeworms caused premature greyness and impotence, and it was said that once they got into the body they were very difficult to expel.

There was great fear of a tapeworm that entered the body while one slept on a certain night in the lunar month called the 'Koshin Night'. This tapeworm, referred to as Amanjaku, would then report on the same night to the God in Heaven about the thoughts and deeds of the persons in whose bodies he resided. And he'd usually do this in a very evil and ill-intentioned way. To prevent this, credulous Japanese did not sleep at all on the Koshin night and they did all they could to keep their children awake until the dawn. This night occurred towards the end of the sixty nights in the sexagesimal cycle, and it was believed that one could subdue the divine tapeworm forever by staying awake seven consecutive times on the Koshin night. Since Amanjaku only reported on that night, the villagers started to make offerings of food and drink to him from about nine o'clock that evening until the dawn. They hoped he'd get so overcome with the feasting that he couldn't get around to making his reports that night, the only night available for him to do so. This custom, related to certain Chinese Taoist practices, still forms a part of village life here and there throughout Japan.

There was also a belief, inherited from the Chinese, in a Koshin God who guarded the fate of all beings. This belief probably came into Japan from China in about the ninth century. Palace ladies and officials composed poems, drank wine, and sang on the Koshin Night, waiting for the dawn, and this became an important festival conducted under imperial auspices. Though at first observed strictly, it gradually evolved into an occasion for drinking, music, and profligation.

In ancient times, in China as well as Japan, there were many days in the month during which sexual intercourse was strictly prohibited. *Couples were warned that the children of such unions would inevitably be inhuman and unfilial. As mentioned earlier, the *Koshin* day was ordained as particularly off limits to sex. Conceiving on this day would result without fail, one was warned, in a child who on reaching adulthood would be evil and felonious. In later times, people did not stay up throughout the night to guard against the malevolent tapeworm but instead said special 'charm words' to prevent its entering their bodies. These words, a magic combination of Sanskrit, Chinese, and Japanese, advised the parasites to sleep and remain dormant. Some Hindu and Buddhist elements got mixed in with the Japanese conception of the *Koshin* taboo, giving rise to the erection of frightful and demoniacal-looking statues that intimidated the on looker from every direction.

BUTTOCKS-TAPPING AND CONCEPTION

There was a folk belief throughout Japan that the woman who tapped the buttocks of a female stone image could become pregnant as a consequence. In Kagoshima, a polished stone shaped like a vagina was conveyed by children to the homes of newlyweds, and the children would then call out the bride and tap her on the buttocks. A similar custom was observed in Shizuoka, with a verbal accompaniment to the effect that 'next year you will give birth to a son'. The stick used for striking the buttocks had a special name. There was a practice of beating promiscuous women in Japanese shrines while these women repented to the gods because of the men they had known carnally during the year in question. The head of the shrine might beat the sexually-indulgent female with a wooden stick called 'a cane of virtuous wood'. This practice must have developed into an inextricable blend of religious faith and sexual excitation, even though total degeneration of the practice into lewd behaviour is not explicitly recorded. There is a remnant of the custom in the form of a 'buttocks-beating festival' held until modern times at a famous shrine in Kyoto.

SEX EMANCIPATION DAY

The ancient Japanese, surrounded by taboos, were allowed one day in the year in which to enjoy uninhibited sexual intercourse.

*Ishihara and Levy, *The Tao of Sex*, pp. 120–27.

On this day, when the sun went down, unmarried girls and wives assembled in their courtyards, awaiting men. The evening's activities began with song, continued with wine and feasting, and concluded with indiscriminate sexual coupling. 'My wife is with another man, and I too am with another man's wife.' At this juncture, the unmarried sought out mates and the married sought to invigorate their sex lives through union with the unknown. While it may have originated as a palace custom, 'Sex Emancipation Day' was practised in Japan until the mid-nineteenth century, when the Tokugawa era came to a close, signifying the end of Japan's seclusion from the West. There were also many religious occasions on which coitus was simulated in connection with sacred events. At the Horai Temple in Aichi Prefecture, for example, men dressed as hunters carried about a wooden phallus made out of a so-called god wood. Their starting point was the dwelling of an elderly man dressed in red, supposed to represent a woman. At other shrines coitus was either acted out or portrayed through the medium of male and female dolls while rice planting was taking place in the fields. In the Kyoto-Osaka area, intercourse on the wedding night was referred to as a 'festival' (*omatsuri*), indicating again the association of sexual intercourse and pseudo-religious observance.

PRAYING TO THE GODS OF SEX

The mountain gods were prayed to for fertility, and in Shiga Prefecture one was forbidden to enter a certain mountain until the festival to the mountain god had come to an end. This was an old custom, with prayers to the god recorded as far back as the late twelfth century. Offerings to the god consisted of wooden phalluses in adult and child sizes; simple congratulatory words were said and wine was drunk. Devotees tried in this way to secure a guarantee from the god that the mountain would remain untroubled for the coming year. It was believed that the mountain god became a god of the fields in the spring, reverting to the role of mountain god upon completion of the autumn harvest.

YOMI LAND AND GOD BODIES

During Japan's Stone Age, stone implements used in prayer represented male and female sex organs, the god bodies of sex. Sex gods signified to the ancients a productive, positive aspect, equated with worship of the life force and with growth. According to the eighth-century classic of the origin of Japan called the *Kojiki* ('Chronicle of Ancient Events'), when the male god Izanagi escaped from the country of Yomi, soldiers born from the body of the female god Iznami tried to kill him. However, with the assistance of a peach branch he expelled his would-be murderers. (The peach branch was revered in Japan as a symbol of protection.) When the Japanese scholar Ota Saburo cited this story, however, he conjectured that the peach seed represented the vagina and signified procreation, with the fuzz on the peach and the female pubic hair regarded as one. The association of peach and vagina, based on similarity of form, is widespread. In Italian, based on resemblance, the word for fig (*fica*) can also mean the vagina, and it forms part of an Italian charm said to be efficacious in expelling demons.* Ancient Chinese classics alleged that the peach could control or kill devils.

THE TACHIKAWA SECT

Towards the end of the Heian era (mid-eleventh century), a sect in the Tachikawa area was started by a very astute priest who argued that the true way of enlightenment was achieved through recourse to sexual lust. He expounded a theory of sexual emancipation, somewhat reminiscent of the Taoist sexologists in China whose doctrines were disseminated among the Japanese at court late in the tenth century. The priest lectured fearlessly on this sex-to-religion theme, advocating the achievement of Buddhahood through male-female intercourse. A Japanese diarist wrote that the founder of this sect, known as Ninkan, was born in 1057 at Kyoto. Ninkan was exiled to Izu for having tried to usurp a brother's position. Realising he could not return to Kyoto, he studied exotic practices and founded his Tachikawa School, the religion of sex. He lived in a chaotic era, with the power of the Fujiwara clan in decline and local military rulers asserting provincial control. His sexual doctrines satisfied the search for happiness in those troubled times and they were easily accepted. The illiterate masses especially embraced this doctrine, further expounded by Ninkan's successor, Monkan, who also regulated the teaching along Tibetan tantric lines. The sect flourished

*Mr Giovanni Palozzolo informs me that Italians of all classes tend to call sex organs by the names of fruits.

110

throughout Japan, depending on three sutras and decreeing that the way to Buddhahood was through lust for women and the cultivation of one's carnal appetites. The leaders of the sect advised against overindulgence in sex and food but declared that a certain amount of each was essential to salvation. 'In the world of desire, there are food, sleep, and lust, but of these three (aspects) one reaches extreme pleasure (only) through lust. The whole universe has been produced from the joining of male and female elements, with everything divided into two aspects, just as humans are divided into male and female. The key to this religion was a belief that the human heart was rooted in sex, and that nirvana was to be reached through a joining of the male and female roots of the human heart.

Its practitioners, having first fasted and purified themselves, entered secret quarters filled with incense. Firmly closing the gates, they intoned the sutras and meditated before male and female gods while locked in sexual embrace. The man thought of the second of the eight patriarchs of the Shingon sect, the woman of a Hindu deva, and they each fell into the illusion of ecstasy. Their spirits reached a separate realm beyond thought and reflection, and they achieved final victory, in the sense of having transcended the mundane realm and the life-death cycle. Here coitus itself was interpreted as a kind of death, with love enabling the practitioner to see for a split second into the nature of death and physical decay. Sexual love and death are still closely associated in Japan, with women uttering exclamations involving death at the height of passion,* but the Tachikawa sect believers posited a final moment in which sex transcended death and 'one quietly looked towards the gates of love'. Similar teachings were propounded by the Nichiren Buddhist sect in ancient times, to the effect that in the realm of sexual intercourse distress was to be equated with enlightenment, life and death of the erectile penis with nirvana.

The Tachikawa Sect, closely related to Tibetan Tantrism, therefore exalted sex as being central to enlightenment. The stress on sexual enjoyment was totally alien to established Buddhist religious practices, and as a sect it was derided as unorthodox in structure and wrong in conception. Its commentaries on specific sutras were not acceptable to the mainstream of Buddhist interpretation, for it deified sex and magnified the role of intercourse in the quest for nirvana. Man and woman prayed before three

---

*Cf. Miyatake Gaikotsu, *Jakumetsu iraku ko*, Tokyo, ca. 1930, a study of the exclamations Japanese women make when they have orgasms. (The late R. H. Van Gulik cited this treatise, but as of May, 1971, I have not been able to locate it.)

boxes, each one of which fit into the other. The innermost box contained one head-bone from a virgin and a white silk cloth which had been dipped nine times into the first menstrual blood of a virgin. Male semen was then placed on the top of the three layers of boxes. The couple might lay down on a very large paper on which was depicted the male and female in sexual congress. The man conceived of himself as a male god, the woman assumed the identity of a goddess, and through their holy intercourse they endeavoured to transcend the confines of this world and arrive at one of the Buddhist realms beyond. The detailed doctrines of the sect, which were transmitted from priest to disciple, were veiled in obscurities and extremely difficult to comprehend. Menstrual-red symbolised the woman, semen-white the man, and the religion posited a development of the foetus into human form in a five-week period.

BUDDHIST CONCEPTS EQUATING WOMAN WITH SIN

The Buddhists believed that woman was incriminated by her very nature, with the degree of her criminal tendencies controlled by the heat of her girdle. There are aged Japanese women who still think this way, accepting Buddhist anti-feminine prejudices. The Buddhists regarded a woman's menstrual period as unclean, and she was required to cleanse herself for seven days afterwards. In Buddhist terms, the propensity of women was towards evil, lewd-ness, and licentiousness; her road to salvation was through religion She had to depend on the holy canon, intoning sutras to draw her away from the path of her natural inclination towards evil and sin. There were many stories of women consumed by jealousy and females who transformed themselves into snakes and other forms of animal life. To achieve Buddhahood, it was incumbent on a woman, no matter how religious she was, to first be trans-formed into a man. So we see that it was impossible for a woman to achieve Buddhahood as long as she was plagued by a woman's body – this is clearly indicated in the sutras.

Woman also could not achieve Buddhahood in her female form because one of the thirty-two marks of Buddhahood was a huge horselike phallus concealed within the Buddha's body. It was supposedly difficult even for males to achieve Buddhahood with-out the so-called horse penis. The ancient Japanese associated god and penis, birth and vagina, aware that all of mankind was 'born from a two-by-four-inch hole, and (on death) entered a two-by-four-foot hole.'

XIII. Traditional Ways In Which Women Were Tortured

The comments which follow are based on the outstanding research of Dr. Inoue Kazuo, an expert on Japanese law who devoted forty years of study to the general subject of Japanese torture and its implications. He published the results of his findings in Japanese in 1969, in a monograph which has already undergone many printings.* His work is recommended without reservation for all who read Japanese. Professor Inoue outlined the history of torture in Japan until the Meiji era (1868), stressing cruelties involving maltreatment of the flesh and including vivid illustrations.

From 1627 to 1631, when Christians were martyred at the 'hot spring hells' of Kyushu, they were stripped naked, tied with ropes, and lowered into the boiling sulphuric hot springs at Unzen Park. In 1629, one of the sixty-four Christians so tortured was a nineteen-year-old virgin. She had earlier swallowed a strong poison in broth which failed to kill her, although it did cause her skin to peel away. Two large stones were placed on her neck, round stones were put on her head, and boiling water was poured on the raw flesh of her shoulders and breasts. She survived sixteen days of this torture.

Pre-Heian laws such as those contained in the Taika Reforms of 645 decreed beating convicts on the shoulders and buttocks but exempted pregnant wives and women who had given birth less than a hundred days before. During the Christian persecutions, Christian women were told that since they were like whores they would be raped in front of a large assemblage unless they renounced their religion. There is one record of a rape of Christian women being carried out before a large group of onlookers, but in general this amounted to no more than a coercive threat.

*Inoue Kazuo, Zankoku no Nihonshi ('A History of Cruel Japan'), Tokyo, Kobunsha 1969, postface by Professor Marius Jansen.

Religious thought and Japanese torture were deeply interwoven, with torture techniques, influenced greatly by Buddhist depictions of the many hells into which the sinful and immoral would be cast after death. There was, for example, a religious hell for those convicted of adultery. Female phantoms bewitched these prisoners of hell, and when the fascinated male got close to the woman she ripped him open with her iron claws. These phantoms would persist in their allurement, causing the profligate captive to be pained endlessly by his lustful thoughts. He might also be chased by women between iron mountains or crushed beneath an iron pestle. This Buddhist hell gravely threatened the adulterer, although in real life the society preserved a double standard, so that the male adulterer was immune from punishment, except from the irate householder he had cuckolded. But the errant wife was dealt with harshly. '

There were sixteen subsidiary Buddhist hells for lechers as well as a hell for drunkards, especially those who adulterated wine with water. Priests who violated nuns or other priests were to suffer upon death the punishment of the fiery hell tenfold. The entire skin of the body was to be stripped off, after which they would be stretched across a scorching surface while molten metal was dissolved and poured down on them.

The so-called stone embracing torture was used chiefly against maidservants and prostitutes. While not officially sanctioned, it was often carried out. The hands and feet of the woman were bound, and a common stone used in pickling vegetables was placed on the woman's knees. She was made to 'embrace' this for hours at a time. There was another torture called the 'offertory box', in which the female prisoner was forced to sit on the serrated edges of the narrow opening in religious coin boxes. In another torture, called the 'wooden horse', she was placed on a pointed wooden surface, with both hands bound behind her. With the lower part of her body nude, she was forced to mount the wooden horse, seated on the sharp raised edge of the wood. A rope was tied around her wrists, and she was made to rise and fall on the sharply pointed wood and to slide along the sharpened edge. This sometimes resulted in a ripping open of the crotch. This torture was extremely painful, for it was excruciating for the woman to straddle the edged wood, even without being raised or lowered. It was an especially cruel torture for modest Japanese women who, in addition to suffering intense pain, were further mortified at having their private parts exposed.

If a woman was suspected of having committed a crime, she might be subjected to being bitten by a poisonous snake. If this snakebite did not poison her system and result in her death, she was then deemed innocent. The snake was regarded in religious terms as a divine messenger who conveyed the intent of the gods. This primitive way of determining guilt or innocence was practised from Japanese antiquity to the days of Shogun Toyotomi Hideyoshi (early seventeenth centuries).

Another kind of snake torture involving women was administered occasionally from the fifteenth to seventeenth centuries. Young female convicts or Christians were placed in a tub full of snakes, the snakes having been purposely allowed to become ravenously hungry. Hot water was poured into the tub and the snakes were struck at the same time, making them react violently. They rolled against the woman's body, biting at her flesh, and finally entered her body through the vagina, continuing to bite as they did so, The scholar who cited these facts drew an analogy with a Japanese side dish in which one mixed live earthworms with beancurd, cooking both together. When the water was heated, the earthworms had no alternative other than to seek a cooler place, so they would dive into the midst of the soft beancurd. In a similar way, the snakes who had no escape from the hot water being poured on them sought somewhere to conceal their bodies and dove into the woman's private parts. Small insects like mosquitoes were also used. A woman could be stripped naked for having committed adultery or for having refused a command from a male in authority to bed down with him. Her body was then immersed in wine, after which she had to endure a night of being enveloped by tiny insects. The mosquitoes were drawn by the odour of the wine and they swarmed around the naked flesh, attacking everywhere. Since hands and feet were bound, the woman was unable to put up the slightest resistance; finally her body became covered with swellings and she lost consciousness.

The technique of the ant torture was about the same, but it differed from the mosquito torture in that the life of the victim was endangered. The ant torture was especially prevalent in Southeast Asia and Africa, with swarms of ants crawling over the victims. The ants, enveloping the coveted flesh *en masse*, did so with such force that they could devour a great elephant right down to the bones. One does not find any record of the ant torture in Japan, although use was made of worms from rotted corpses.

The victim was placed in their midst, and it was said that the fierce and evil smell proved unbearable to the victim's senses. There are also medieval records of victims being forced to eat excrement.

Oaths sworn at the moment of death were remembered and feared. There was a famous incident concerning a prostitute exiled to the distant island of Hachiyoshima when she was only fifteen. The girl, known as Tomikiku, continued her profession on the island, having sex in her hut with many of her fellow exiles. In that way she eked out a living by the only means of livelihood she knew. Being prettier than any other woman on the island, she gradually gained favour and influence. After having lived there for almost twenty-five years, Tomikiku joined six other conspirators in trying to escape by boat, but three drowned and the remaining four were captured. The three men with her were tortured to death, but she was spared torture and instead was sentenced to be shot. On the way to the execution grounds, she applied make-up, stood up bravely amidst the ropes that bound her, and hopped about before the execution squad. Hit by a bullet in the chest, the dying woman swore an oath that on her death she would become a poisonous insect and bite them all. 'Look out! There will be vengeance, never fear!' she cried.* That year, when a great insect pestilence was suffered at Hachiyoshima, the insects were called 'Otomi insects'.

Still another prostitute named Hanashima escaped from Hachiyoshima with her lover in 1841, but both of them were captured ninety days later. The man then wrote a diary in jail in which he described how convicts were also executed at Hachiyoshima by having their heads smashed in with a huge axe.† Hanashima's lover was finally pardoned, but he died of a lung ailment less than a month after his release. Exile to Hachiyoshima, incidentally, was regarded as only one degree less severe than the death penalty. It was not until 1882 that the punishment of exile was abolished.

REVENGE BY CUCKOLDED HUSBANDS

For almost four centuries, from the beginning of the Warring States era (1488) to the end of the Yedo era (1867), the adulterous wife and her lover could be summarily dealt with by the aggrieved

*Zankoku no Nihonshi, pp. 130–32.
†Ibid., p. 133, q.v.

husband. His right to decapitate both parties was publicly recognised. It was also technically permissible for him to cut wife and lover each into four parts, severing their nose, fingers, and sex organs as he pleased. But no one other than the husband was allowed to do this. Adulterous criminals could also be publicly prosecuted. In feudal Japanese society, adultery by the female was considered an extremely serious crime because of the importance given to preserving the correct blood lineage. The husband was legally permitted to kill both wife and lover until 1870, when this form of adultery became punishable by three years of exile for each of the guilty parties. In modern Japan this is no longer a crime, but it is considered valid grounds for divorce.

THE BROTHEL QUARTERS AS A REALM OF SUFFERING

An earlier chapter entitled 'The History of Prostitution in Japan' described how in feudal times young girls might be sold into prostitution by their impoverished parents. Some of these girls were as young as ten years old. They were thereupon forced into serving the best part of their lives as captive playthings of the male. In the Yedo era (1603-1867), for example, a large number of poor farm girls were sold into prostitution. It is a matter of historical record that, on first becoming a prostitute, the girl might be incarcerated in a basket, there to be treated worse than the lowest beast. Any man could rape her as he pleased, so maltreating her that she suppressed her feelings and evolved into a woman whose sexual organs were so maltreated that she couldn't bear children. She was controlled with severity, and if caught while trying to escape she was immediately bound with ropes by a bodyguard and cruelly punished. The playwright Chikamatsu and the novelist Saikaku wrote in detail of the chastisement of the whore. The quarters were self-regulatory, and those who broke the rules had to silently endure arbitrary punishments. When a prostitute left the quarters for personal reasons and without permission, she was usually penalised by being confined in a large inverted tub which had one small window in it, with a large rock placed on top. Or if she failed to draw customers for several days, she might be whipped. Other penalties included her being bound in the nude with ropes on which water was poured, to be further injured as the water penetrated the ropes; being made to go without food for several days; and being forced to eat on a full stomach. There were examples of women punishing women, often in wild and hysterical

117

ways. The worst penalties were meted out to would-be escapees and to would-be suicides, because either flight or suicide were injurious to the interests of the brothel owner. The prostitute who took away another's regular customer could, upon deliberation by the other prostitutes, be cruelly punished. Whores in the depths of sadness and despair had no other way out than to hang themselves or throw themselves down wells. They were then buried in unmarked graves.

Kameyu was a famous beauty who lived towards the end of the Tokugawa shogunate, a woman who had gone into the Yoshiwara at the age of eleven in order to assist her sick parents financially. She was serving at Yokohama's Gankiro when an American, admiring her superlative beauty, tried to buy her out of the quarters. Kameyu resisted this purchase, but she was ordered to go with the buyer at the insistance of the master. This she did, only to commit suicide at the first opportunity.

There were young girls in the quarters called *kamuro*, usually about ten to thirteen years of age, who served the older women. The *kamuro* had to sweep and clean the rooms and also learn how to sing, dance, and play the samisen. In addition, they were taught to read, arrange flowers, and partake in the tea ceremony. Failure to learn resulted in beatings and starvation. The *kamuro* would be beaten with a small lit smoking pipe (called *kiseru*) until their feet became numb and their knees gave way under them. They were often shut up in solitary confinement by the prostitutes whom they had to serve; there is one record of a *kamuro* who had coins heated by candles poured into her mouth until she died of suffocation. She was said to have left a mark on the white wall in her death agonies which could never be erased. The woman who had killed this *kamuro* was so disturbed by her vengeful ghost that she took ill and died less than a month afterwards. The alternatives to obsequious obedience were so drastic that most of the prostitutes endured the regime of the quarters and became full-fledged professionals. While most of these women were sold by their parents, in earlier times some were probably slaves sold by their owners during war and civil upheaval.

When legal prostitution was outlawed in Japan in the postwar period (1958), the former quarters of opulent prostitution went into sharp economic decline, to be replaced by other forms of the same commerce.

Possession by the devil has been a belief in Japan since ancient times, very similar to the belief of the Chinese. It involves foxes, badgers, snakes, and other animals believed to be manifestations of spirits that come back to plague man in human form. When two foxes that were mates had a quarrel, it was alleged, the female killed the male and ate his intestines. Stories involving beautiful women who were foxes in disguise are legion, and there were said to be families possessed by foxes in which the fox protected the family line and brought evil to those the family disliked. In the Izumi region, families possessed by foxes were called 'black', those not so possessed were called 'white'. White and black families did not intermarry or attend one another's funerals. This Izumi superstition may have arisen as late as the mid-Tokugawa era (ca. 1750) as a restriction against immigrants. It was later officially prohibited, but it is said to have its covert adherents to the present day.

XIV. Infanticide

An agronomist of the Tokugawa era named Sato Shinen commented in one of his works that pregnant women in all poor countries who cannot afford to rear any more children secretly induce abortions. In another work, he cited poverty as the main cause of infanticide as well as abortion.

Infanticide was most commonly practised in farming and fishing villages located north of the Kanto Plain. Other areas where infanticide also flourished were cited by Japanese writers on this subject, one economist stating that it prevailed from the Hakone Mountain passes to the Azuma region. Hiei Shrine in Gumma Prefecture has preserved an unusual anti-infanticide song and a votive picture, the picture showing a midwife murdering the newborn child by breaking its legs and smothering it. Behind the midwife is mirrored another woman's face, with two horns protruding from the forehead. This female demon's eyes are glittering fiercely, and its mouth extends as far back as the ears. The illustration is intended to prove that the heart of a woman who practices infanticide is really that of an evil demon. This kind of votive picture was probably once displayed throughout Japan.

Infanticide was referred to by euphemistic terms such as 'to return' or 'to frolic in the mountains'. The methods of killing unwanted infants included crushing, strangling, smothering, and burying alive. It was believed that disaster would befall the practitioner. One work stated that it was simple to kill kittens and puppies but not infants, for it was feared that the homes of infant-murderers would collapse in ruins. So these infants were probably killed out of sheer desperation, the real cause being starvation and near-disastrous economic conditions.

Peasant women of the Tokugawa age tried to induce abortions and prevent births by any and all primitive means available to them. After intercourse, the woman might hop about on one leg five or six times, and later, if pregnant, she might shake her body to try to induce miscarriage. Other techniques were for the pregnant woman to drink vinegar, eat red peppers, cuttlefish, or ground rose seeds, and to try striking the sex organs with a tree root. Even if she endangered her life, she would do anything conceivable to prevent a normal birth. Parents who wished whole-heartedly to have no further children might call an infant by such names as 'Stop', 'The Last One', and 'Shut Off'. If they had twins, they would often keep one infant and kill the other. The reason they gave was that giving birth to twins or triplets was animal-like, similar to a dog or another four-legged beast's giving birth to a litter. In Kochi Prefecture, two boys and one girl in the family were considered ideal, and infants above that number were likely to be killed. Regardless of wealth, inhabitants in Tosa were ashamed to have more than three children.

There were many official proclamations against infanticide, but they failed to be effective, and from 1676 to 1787 there was a marked decrease in the agrarian population. The history of infanticide in Japan reflects the economic hardships and the harsh political rule which the peasants suffered during much of the Tokugawa era (1603-1867).

Appendices: Sex and Today's Japan

I. THE VIRGINITY HANG-UP OF THE JAPANESE

The man-woman relationship in postwar Japan has changed in many ways, enough to give rise to the term 'sexual revolution', but the Japanese male still wants to be sure that his bride is a virgin. He talks a lot about 'free sex', but when he signs up for matrimony he'll try to marry a virgin every time. Here we've got a real conflict of the sexes, for the unwed girl who's in love has to soberly reflect on her future options before she gives in to her lover and surrenders her most priceless possession. First she's afraid that once she does, her lover will tire of her and turn to another woman. In other words, she'll lose her virginity and his love besides. But then there's that very down-to-earth and practical consideration of what the loss entails. She's hounded by conscience: 'Even though the pain in your heart is cured with the passage of time, as a non-virgin won't you be spurned by a true marriage partner when one appears? You feel uneasy about giving your body to your lover because of the calamitous portent that it foretells.'

One Japanese sexologist believes that the Japanese male outlook on virginity is the same now as it was in prewar days. He contrasts Japan and England, saying that almost half of the British males think it's all right for a girl to have premarital intercourse, but that only *one per cent* of their Japanese counterparts take the same affirmative position. And only 11.8 per cent of the Japanese men he interviewed said that they didn't care whether or not their brides were virgins. (These figures were given in a Japanese weekly, in an article called 'Sex Knowledge of the Japanese'.)

There was the case, for example, of a girl operated on for hymen restoration at the Ginza Hospital of Plastic Surgery in Tokyo. She was twenty-one. A man had promised to marry her, and she had sex relations with him for more than a year before discovering that he had a wife. He offered to divorce his wife, but she turned him down out of empathy for the other woman. Half a year after

121

they'd broken up, she started going with a young bachelor who proposed marriage, and that was when she started thinking about restoring her hymen. She told the hospital director that she was doing this to avoid hurting her fiance.

Reverence for a woman's virginity was part and parcel of Japan in the old days of feudalism and militarism. Then the prime purpose of marriage was to transmit to posterity one's family name, status, and property. Japan's feudal leaders believed in a 'pure blood' doctrine, and they refused to tolerate the slightest suspicion that the new-born child belonged to any man other than the husband. Medical knowledge in old Japan was rudimentary, and fornication was associated with mental illness and leprosy. The man who wived a woman with a record of premarital sex was afraid she'd diffuse poisonous diseases into his family line. The lower classes were not rigid proponents of virginity like their military rulers, and in farming and fishing villages there were communal sleep-ins at lodgings set up for free love exchanges between single youths and maidens. But even when feudal Japanese society crumbled in 1868, the ruling class was still made up of people with military class backgrounds. There was a rush to imitate the West, but European moralists in those days also esteemed virginity, so the restraints on female sexuality remained.

But in modern Japan medical knowledge is widespread, as are techniques for avoiding pregnancy and contagious diseases. The rationale for confining female sexuality has disintegrated, and with the disintegration one might expect to find an about-face in the value placed on virginity. But such is not yet the case. For two days in February, 1970, the editorial board of a popular Japanese journal interviewed fifty-one men in two sections of Tokyo known as Shinjuku and Ginza, asking them to reply to this question:

'Do you place a value on the so-called woman's virginity?'

Thirty-two of the fifty-one men replied that they did, giving a few simple reasons why. (Nineteen of the thirty-two 'virginity advocates' were bachelors.) They said things like, 'New goods are undeniably the best. When television sets and wristwatches become used, even if you bring them to a pawnshop you'll get a cheap price for them.' That was how a 19 year-old student expressed himself; a student two years his senior remarked: 'A nonvirgin female has leisurely gone about sexual experimentations with other men, and that gives me an unclean feeling.' A 27 year-old worker in a publishing firm alleged that virgins in Japan were to be valued because they were so rare: 'Up to now I've never met one.' A businessman also in his late twenties used a commercial simile: 'You know that when a car is used it means that it's got accustomed to the way that someone else handles it.' And a 23 year-old company employee exalted the virgin in these terms: 'The girl who preserves her virginity has proved she has a steadfast nature.' A married man in his mid-thirties made this conjecture about female psychology: 'Regardless of what the man thinks, today's woman realises that once she loses her virginity she becomes "defective merchandise". Of course that's knowledge she conceals in her innermost heart.' The nineteen men who saw no value in female virginity tended to express themselves more in terms of equality of the sexes, in contrast to the proponents of virginity who equated marriage with property ownership. The nineteen said things like, 'The heart is more important than the flesh'; 'In love, anything goes.' 'The hymen is of no use.' 'The non-virgin woman is no trouble and she can be more easily enjoyed.'

The editorial staff of the Japanese journal was surprised by the preponderance of old ways of thinking, since they had conducted their interviews in the parts of Tokyo widely regarded as extremely progressive. They decided to probe further through hypnotic analyses, this time selecting 13 married men, aged twenty to thirty. First they held a round-table discussion, at which only five of the thirteen admitted from the outset that they esteemed virginity. But after chatting back and forth for three hours, a consensus was arrived at to the effect that, 'If you're going to take a wife, she really should be a virgin!' Three of the married participants agreed to undergo hypnosis, the results of which proved that these men valued virginity but suspected otherwise of their wives. This may reflect in part the availability to Japanese women of a hymen-restoring operation, done simply and for about a hundred dollars, in which the broken membrane is stitched together to give a deceptive impression to the male.

The operation itself is evidence of 'double standard' thinking in Japan, with woman's sexuality sacrificed to male lust. The words used to describe the loss of female virginity refer to her 'giving', 'offering up', and 'allowing'. She's also referred to as having been dirtied, plundered, or abandoned. So she's traditionally placed in a straight jacket of passivity, her sexuality arrested within a male-directed framework. The Japanese woman is now striving for liberation through the unhampered exploration of her own special needs, and as she achieves improved economic and social status she should be increasingly regarded by the male as an equal partner and not as passive property for him to manipulate in egoistic disregard of her sexual needs.

II. FIRST-CLASS JAPANESE OFFICE GIRLS
ARE 90.2 PER CENT PURE!

A one-man crusader named Koichi Shiraishi has been trying to find out how virginity fares in the midst of Japan's so-called sex revolution. He originally sent questionnaires to unmarried women working as shop employees, waitresses, and company clerks; almost one-quarter of the 1,547 respondents revealed that they were no longer virgins. He then decided to interview women employed by first-class firms in the Tokyo and Osaka areas, and in the early spring of 1970 made known the results of this second investigation.* Less than ten per cent of the 1,676 women answered affirmatively that they were sexually experienced, indicating that in Japan first rank companies have the most virgins.

The girls who are no longer virgins got sexually involved for a variety of reasons. A 25 year-old bank employee, for example, told of how she let herself be seduced by a bank depositor known to her only by face and name. He invited her to a tea-house, she accepted, and from there they went to a hotel.

'Did you like him especially well?'

'No, it wasn't a case of liking him or of disliking him.'

'Why did such a mood come over you?'

'I don't know, but I'd always wanted to become an adult, so I tried it out.'

A 22 year-old employee in 'M' Company said that she belonged to a group in which everyone indulged in sex. A 24 year-old clerk in a construction company said that she yielded to her lover after he made five or six advances because it was too bothersome to do otherwise. Another young respondent said that the girls in her company were all very sex conscious, but that they'd never admit this to one another out of fear of being considered immoral. One girl thought that the third year of work was the time when virginity was most imperilled. The first year she got adjusted to the company the second year she got interested in her work, but by the third year the work bored her and she yearned for excitement.

Most of the girls had first sex experiences with lovers, but a significant minority surrendered virginities to chance acquaintances, entering into the relationship casually and regarding sex as a kind of sport. They had intercourse mainly in hotels, motels, and automobiles, the latter being used only since the end of World War II. One girl in her early twenties said that when she refused

*See *Young Lady*, March, 1970, pp. 122–6, the Japanese journal from which the following information is summarised.

to go all the way with her boy friend, they had a big quarrel. The next day she dated a fellow-employee and gave up her virginity in a nearby hotel. She said she'd been motivated by a desire for revenge.

Passion was the main reason given for the first intercourse. But once the girls experienced this, many of them had sex with other men as well, showing a shift away from the Confucian idea that the woman who gives herself to a man should remain his and only his for all times. One girl, for example, admitted that she gave herself first to a man insensitive to her feelings and then to a man interested in her only as a sex object. Now she was enjoying sex with a third man. Some of the Japanese women interviewed in this transitional era equated passion with free love and declared that the old arranged marriage was anathema to love. It was love they wanted, the love that might lead to a perfect marriage. The virgin made much of the significance of the first sex act, but the non-virgin tended to minimise it and to play down its consequences.

The overwhelming majority of first-class company women want to keep their virginities until they marry. Mr Shiraishi interprets this as based not on morality but on calculation, with each female wanting to maintain an effective bargaining position. One woman admitted she let her boy-friend freely kiss her but resisted him fiercely when he tried to go all the way, for to her virginity was to be the monopoly of her future husband. Other women likewise regarded the premarital loss of virginity as an irreparable loss. Mr Shiraishi is now convinced that the old ideas of virtue and morality that Japanese women once held are being replaced by a profit-and-loss concept in which the woman regards her hymen as a highly marketable commodity, to be reserved for the marriage bidder.

III. THREE'S NO CROWD TO JAPANESE NEWLYWEDS

Whether they marry for love or by arrangement, the major problem facing newlyweds in Japan is usually that of crowded quarters and thin walls. They can easily hear and be heard by their next-door neighbours. About half of Japan's newlyweds will live in apartments, often flimsily built structures. Let's take, for example, the case of a Tokyo couple in their mid-twenties who started married life two Februaries ago in a one room efficiency, adjoined to a tiny kitchen. They rent this for 13,000 yen (about $36) monthly. The husband is a salesman whose salary fluctuates, helped out by his wife who works in an office. Their combined monthly income ranges from about $150 to $200. The landlord occupies all of the first floor, while they live in one of four apartments set up on the second floor. The walls are vinyl plastic, with neighbours on either side clearly heard. The four families share the use of one toilet. Their windows are lower than those of their neighbours, so they always have to draw their curtains to avoid being seen. The wife admits that she never realised her dreams of wedded bliss would turn into a nightmare because of the harsh reality of sub-standard living facilities. When night falls, the stereo set from the neighbour on the left and the TV from the neighbour on the right may start up full blast, signifying that the men have returned home and raised the volume to conceal the sounds of lovemaking. And when the lovemaking ends, the couples have to get dressed to go to the toilet, to avoid the embarrassment of being seen by others in love's disarray. The wife yearns for an apartment with thick walls and a private toilet – how many million Tokyoites share her yearnings?

In Japan the husband's parents often move in with the newly-weds. The following case study involves a 23 year-old wife, her 27 year-old husband, and the husbands' mother.* They live in three rooms, the mother-in-law in a room opposite that of the newly-weds. When they first got married, there wasn't even a sliding door between the rooms; when the wife requested one, the husband replied that it wasn't needed since, after all, they were a married couple. But she finally got her way and had one installed, only to have her mother-in-law take it down in the summer and replace it with a flimsy rattan blind, saying it was cooler that way. The wife suffered cruelly from the lack of privacy. She could hear every sound her mother-in-law made, and even at the height of sexual climax she was afraid to make the slightest noise.

The tensions brought on by insufferably cramped housing conditions in Japan sometimes burst forth in headlines of suicides and homicides. A population study made in 1966 revealed that the average age for marriage was twenty-seven for the man, twenty-four for the woman. One of six bridegrooms in the 25-29 year range owned his own home, one of five rented a home, and one of ten lived in a home provided by his company, but forty-five per cent rented apartments like the ones we've just described. So almost half of Japan's newlyweds must be living in crowded

*See *Josei jishin* (a popular Japanese magazine), March, 1970, pp. 74–8, for this case study and the other information cited in my article.

quarters, unable to freely enjoy sexual pleasures because they are unable to afford privacy and seclusion. The new concrete apartment buildings allow much greater privacy than the older wooden structures, but they're often in the suburbs, requiring two hours of commuting time to and from work. Someone has estimated the number of calories used up during two hours of commuting as three times the amount needed for sexual intercourse; how would New York suburbanites rate in a similar survey?

The stresses and strains of newlyweds in cramped quarters can lead to frigidity or impotence. There was, for example, the medical case of a 28 year-old man being treated for sexual impotence. He, his wife, and his mother lived in the same apartment, and every time he was getting ready to have sexual intercourse his mother would cough and come into his bedroom under the pretext of having forgotten something there. So impotence resulted, an impotence so severe it had to be treated through hypnosis. In a similar way, the newlywed Japanese wife who can't give vent to cries of pleasure during foreplay and sexual climax, cautioned instead by her husband to keep quiet so as not to disturb either his mother or the neighbours, is headed for a mental conflict which may result in frigidity, aversion to sex, or withdrawal symptoms. He or she then become mentally ill, despite their best efforts to put up with impossibly crowded and cramped conditions and to seek wedded sexual bliss in hostile surroundings.

Another shortcoming of the one-room apartment is that husband and wife are never out of sight of one another. There's always a danger that the lack of privacy will eventually kill desire, as the couple are unable to draw a curtain around their mundane lives, to be lifted for those special occasions of love and passion. In these circumstances familiarity breeds ennui, as the veils are completely removed and the mysterious and enchanted recede before the prosaic and the commonplace. The further elevation of living standards among the Japanese will probably help solve the problem of adequate housing accomodations, for more and more young Japanese are coming to realise that thin walls and outside toilets inhibit the full and carefree sexual enjoyment they look for in marriage.

IV.   MARRIAGE BY LOVE OR ARRANGEMENT?

Marriages in the East have traditionally been between families rather than individuals, with the matchmaker playing a central role in bringing together prospective brides and grooms of like social status. But the use of the matchmaker in Japan is on a gradual but inevitable decline, and even where his services are requested these days acceptance or rejection of the proposal is usually left to the discretion of the girl.

In March, 1970, a special report on this topic appeared in a popular Japanese magazine under the title. 'Love Marriage or Arranged Marriage?'* The writer first contrasted the intimacy of the love marriage with the calculated sexuality of the union brought to fruition by the matchmaker. Miss Yuriko Sakawa, a 20 year-old office girl, visited a Mrs S, who had married for love. There she was, drinking from her husband's half-finished teacup and saying that doing so was perfectly natural because they were passionately in love. Yuriko recalled how her best friend K, the product of an arranged marriage, had once confessed to her that her husband regarded kissing solely as part of the foreplay for sexual intercourse. Outside of the bedroom she had never been kissed.

A random investigation of a hundred young married women, aged twenty-two to twenty-five, indicates that Japanese today marry for love. (Eighty-four love marriages, eleven arranged marriages, five not clearly one or the other.) However, the chief researcher notes that '. . . when you listen closely, you discover that most of the marriages developed into love through the form of an arranged introduction'. In other words, despite the fact that most of these young wives first met their husbands through arrangements, they so yearn for a love union that initially they repress the unpleasant truth about the arrangement. Exemplifying differences in traditional Eastern and modern Western outlook, it's been said that in the East couples marry and then fall in love, the reverse of Western practice.

But the proponents of arranged marriage in Japan remind us that love marriages may look more appealing on the surface, only to prove inferior in the day-to-day routine of wedded life. First there's the prospect of cooking. The man who marries for love has to grin and bear it no matter how poorly his wife cooks. The bean soup (staple of Japanese breakfasts) may be tasteless, but he didn't marry her for her cooking talents. 'I want you, so anything you cook is OK with me.' If he shows he's displeased with her cooking, then the earlier protestations of love become the meaningless exclamations of an emotional moment. But one of the qualifications of the girl whose marriage is arranged is usually that

*See *Josei jishin*, March, 1970, pp. 60–62.

she can cook well; so the husband may not enjoy as passionate a love but he'll be wined and dined in style.

Then there's the question of the wash. In love marriages, more than a fourth of the men interviewed washed the panties of their wives. Why? One husband explained that, 'It takes just a second to do this in the washing machine, so it's nothing to feel sorry for us about. Women have trouble with switches and meters, so if we men operate the washing machines for them instead it ensures that the machines will last longer.' These words are inconceivable to that husband of an arranged marriage who equates washing machines with wifely duties.

The couple in love find it difficult to get along with their relatives and neighbours. Their intimacy makes them less willing to share in the social amenities required of them in a crowded society where everyone lives in close proximity. Mrs U, who married for love, lives in a small apartment. When her salesman-husband goes to work in the morning, she follows him down the stairs with a parting kiss. She has gone so far as to wash his undergarments in the public baths, a procedure which shocked the local gossips and started neighbourhood rumours. This reaction so infuriated Mrs U that she smashed at a neighbour's door with a trash container, a move ill-designed to foster good relations. In short, the 'love wife' is oblivious to the eyes of those around her. The researcher for the Japanese journal surmised that four-fifths of the women now must be washing their husbands' drawers in the public baths, a clear violation of established mores.

But arranged-marriage couples enjoy associating with neighbours and relatives, and they enter much more easily and without rancour into the social life marked by family visits and social exchange.

There's also the factor of children, often considered a hindrance to the intimacy cherished by the couple in love. But in arranged marriages the children tend to strengthen the husband-wife relationship. As one man remarked, when he and his wife were living with his parents: 'Until then, it was like returning to my parents' home. But with the birth of a child we became a complete family unit. It is a precious existence. Now when I see my wife from the rear, busily preparing dinner, I want to enfold her in my arms. I get the feeling that this love which envelops me is the real thing.'

Then there's the question of the fickleness of the man. Here too the love-marriage male shows a tendency to repeat the cycle of romance and seduction, less willing to adjust to the cooling-off period that sets in with the inroads of time. In an extreme example of this, Shigeko Marui married for love with an office Romeo named Takahashi who wooed her assiduously, taking her out bowling and for long drives. But soon after they wed Takahashi reverted to his bachelor ways, playing around so much with other women that in less than a year the marriage ended up in the divorce courts.

In arranged marriages sex ripens slowly but often surely, reminiscent of the saying that such couples marry first and fall in love afterwards. But in love marriages there's always the danger that boredom will reign after the initial passion palls, in ways that are irredeemable. Mrs. Y married for love, but by the eighth year she discovered to her dismay that her husband was physically avoiding her. And then she discovered the reason. To her shock and humiliation, she found him once vigorously masturbating in his study. She felt insulted, but when she remonstrated with him he coldly replied that he was bored with her body and therefore had to compensate for his boredom through self-induced erotic imaginings.

One marriage counsellor and member of the Tokyo Family Arbitration Commission states that when women come to him to talk of divorce, those who bitterly denounce their husbands are almost all the products of love marriages. But in arranged marriages, since the agreement involves the families of each party, divorces tend to be avoided and problems are more objectively considered. There's more marital stability than in love marriages, since the latter are predicated on the willful interests of the two parties alone and there is a preoccupation with passion, to the detriment of mutual understanding and social awareness.*

V. SEX-SENSITIVITY ZONES OF JAPANESE WOMEN

The enthusiasm for research in Japan has now been extended to sexual studies, such as those conducted in the summers of 1968 and 1969 by the Sexual Psychology Research Institute.† In 1968 the institute questioned a thousand bachelors and a thousand

*How about other aspects of marriage? The questionnaire revealed that the love marriage group generally saves less money, spending large sums on cars and on leisure activities, while the arranged marriage group is more frugal, tending to invest in housing. The women in this latter group suffer many more illnesses involving frigidity and gastro-intestinal obstructions. Those who wed for love suffer more from neuroses. They face the greatest threat of divorce in the first year of marriage, one year earlier than the arranged-marriage wife.

†Cited in the Japanese journal *Shosetsu hoseki*, September, 1969, pp. 66–74, from which I have obtained this information on sex-sensitivity zones.

single girls, aged eighteen to twenty-five, and came up with the startling information that Japanese men kept their virginity longer than Japanese women. More than four-fifths of the males remained virgins till twenty-three, while almost half of the females had their first sex experience at eighteen. Half of the women were attracted to older married men with families, and a third of these were able to have orgasms during intercourse with such men.

One year later, in the summer of 1969, the institute questioned a hundred each of wives, office girls, coeds, and bar and cabaret hostesses, inquiring about their sex lives and their sex-sensitivity zones. Again the factor of young women preferring older men proved significant, as illustrated in the following revelation by Mr T, a playboy in his late thirties. He revealed to institute researchers how he had had an affair with a 19 year-old college student, a young lady short in stature but pretty, smooth-skinned, and well developed in breasts and thighs. Up to that time Mr T had had nothing to do with women under twenty-seven, regarding them as sexually ignorant and marriage-oriented. But Miss Oko, with her extraordinarily good sex techniques, taught him otherwise. She let him fully enjoy the foreplay, kissing with tongues intertwined and then saying to him, 'Now Uncle, please lick the inside of my tongue with yours.' As he did this, she placed his hands on top of her breasts. After pressing them till they got larger, he lightly pinched and pulled them, kissed them, gently bit the nipples, and swung them from left to right with the tip of his tongue. He pressed his lips to her flesh, going from her armpits to the side of her bosom to her pubic area. He stroked her hips and thighs with palms and fingers and moved towards the vagina. Dreamily, and with closed eyes, she then took the initiative, nursing Mr T's penis and performing fellatio on it without the slightest hesitation. They played this way for at least an hour, after which she signalled for him to insert his penis. He did so, there was a trickle of blood, and she confessed that till that night she'd been a true, honest-to-goodness virgin!

How, then, could the virginal Miss Oko have been so well-versed about what to do and how to do it? It's because one characteristic of many of today's young Japanese girls is an extreme enthusiasm about sex research and techniques. Miss Oko, for example, from fifteen to nineteen said that she had engaged in heavy petting with about twenty young men. But she stopped just short of intercourse because she feared that she'd be handled roughly by the young male if she were totally permissive. That's why she wanted to associate with an older and more considerate and understanding male like Mr T, who she affectionately referred to as 'uncle'.

Mr T was astonished by Miss Oko's statement, for it disproved three of his favourite prejudices, namely that:

1. Virgins have a poor sense of orgasm.
2. In foreplay, one concentrates only on breasts and clitoris.
3. Women are strongly influenced by the first male they have sex with.

Mr T discovered that the young Japanese woman of today is much more knowledgeable in sexual techniques than her mother was two decades before.

Sex-Sensitivity Zones, from the Head on Down

Now, starting with the head, let's look at the sex-sensitivity zones. It's often said that a woman's whole body is sexually sensitive; this may be so, but many women interviewed by the Sexual Psychology Research Institute said they were sexually aroused around the head region. Eight per cent preferred to be stroked around the eyes, ears, nose and lips, in addition to lip and tongue stimulation. Let's look at one woman from this group and her revelations: Miss Keiko Negishi, a 21 year-old office worker.

Miss Negishi was raped by her adopted elder brother when she was fifteen, after which she had relations with nineteen men, one after the other. She was now intimate with a 19 year-old student. The thing in common she derived from all these experiences was to have her hair pulled. She was gently stroked at first, after which she strongly intertwined tongues. She felt numb all over if her hair were strongly pulled, the nape of her neck lightly stroked, and the top bones of her spine firmly massaged. Then she wanted to be stroked and kissed from her breasts to her pubic bone and the inside of her thighs. But she told her lovers first that she had to have her hair pulled and the nape of her neck stroked.

The fact that the ears are sexually susceptible to manipulation is well-known. (Statement by bar hostess Midori Suga, twenty-one:) 'If my ears are skilfully manipulated, I always have an orgasm.' First she wants them whispered into with words of desire: feeling the male's breath by her ears enables her to relax. Then she wants her earlobes lightly pulled. A fingernail placed in her ear and then rubbed against it gives her ecstatic pleasure. That's when she implores the man to kiss her eyes. She wants the man to tenderly bite her earlobes, lick the ear, and then insert tongue tip into the aperture. She says this gives her the same sensation as if cunnilingus is being performed on her.

Eyes and Nose

'At first I want my face to be gently stroked, especially the ends of my closed eyes and the tip of my nose. When I feel the inner part of a man's finger below my nose, it seems to set me afire.' This quotation is from Miss Shizuko Yamaoka, a 19 year-old office worker. Her present lover, her only one to date, touched her that way before touching her breasts. She became inordinately fond of having her eyes and nose stroked, aware of pleasurable reactions in breasts and clitoris. After intercourse, she wanted to be lightly kissed above her eyes and to rub noses.

The Nape of the Neck

The ancients also realised that stroking and kissing the neck afforded sexual pleasures, with the term 'necking' a metaphor for foreplay. Almost all women interviewed by the institute admitted to being sensitive there. In fact, 24 year-old waitress Mieko Kubo said she couldn't function sexually without first being caressed about the neck.

Her male pilgrimage had started at twenty, after which she'd been intimate with eight men. Her first lover was a 40 year-old supervisor at the company where she worked. He was strongly built and very skilled in techniques. At their first physical encounter, he kissed her lips and then the nape of her neck below the ears, using lips and tongue rapidly and with immediate effect. Miss Kubo's breasts got larger, she felt as if she were being massaged and undressed at the same time, and when he let his hands move slowly from the top of her knees to the inside of her thighs, she felt so ecstatic that her body seemed to be multiplying itself. After that, foreplay for her had to include ardent caressing of her neck. She let her hair grow long to conceal kiss-marks left there by lovers anxious and willing to please.

Fingers, Arms, and Shoulders

Miss Asako Sakurai was a 27 year-old office worker, a divorcee now living with a 20 year-old college student. What she liked most about her young lover was the devoted services that he rendered. First she lay down and had him play with each of her fingers, lightly biting and kissing the fleshy parts. She let his tongue and lips creep along her palms and the inner flesh of her arms. Then he lightly bit the flesh around her shoulders and moved lowed, using both hands, shifting to bosom and ribs and proceeding from cunnilingus to insertion. This took about thirty minutes. She wanted to take the initiative, but she held back and passively endured his caresses until her entire body was convulsed with pleasure. Miss Sakurai stated that her husband had been impatient and never willing to do any of these things for her.

The Pit of the Stomach

A woman is extremely ticklish at the pit of the stomach because she is so sexually sensitive there. Mrs Yoko Abe, aged twenty-six, said that her shopkeeping husband was the eighth man she'd known sexually but the first one to awaken her femininity. The first night she was with him, he tickled the pit of her stomach most thoroughly, then pressed her down and sadistically stroked her. Her laughter changed to screams, but as he relentlessly charged she felt a sharp sensation of pleasure that took her by surprise. She now was less ticklish but, as he intensified his services, unbearable excitement engulfed her. She required about thirty minutes of foreplay, followed by twenty minutes of intercourse and five or six minutes of postplay. She usually had about five orgasms.

The Breasts

Miss Atsushi Koya, twenty-six and unemployed, was the most unique of the women interviewed by the Sexual Psychology Research Institute. She gave her virginity to a 22 year-old college teacher, but right after that she spent a night in Kyoto with an Italian businessman. And it was the experienced European male who made her aware of what it was to be a woman.

Westerners have a reputation in the East for persistence in foreplay and adeptness in tonguing the breasts, navel, and pubic parts. It's said that they always fondle the breasts, one after the other, while simultaneously engaging in other types of love-play designed to cause complex but harmonious sensations of pleasure to course through the woman's body. When Miss Koya found herself in the amorous hands of the Italian, he touched his tongue to her left nipple, causing it to resolve, and at the same time exerted pressure with his palm on her right nipple. Then he grasped a breast in one hand and soothed her thighs with the other. He also placed his lips lightly over and around her navel, again and again, pushing the tip of his tongue against it as if he were trying to suck up her whole body. Then he lightly bit Miss Koya alongside her breasts, causing her a kind of bittersweet pleasure that finally made her want to convulse with a laughter bordering on hysteria. Of course, during this time he was playing with her vagina in various ways, leisurely consuming almost two hours in elaborate foreplay. Miss Koya had an orgasm in foreplay before she realised it, the memory of which occupied her every thought long afterwards. She'd been so well 'broken in' by her European lover that now she needed at least three hours of sexual dalliance to obtain satisfaction. Her present lover was a middle-aged company director, whose touch was in no way inferior to that of the Italian. She had intercourse four times monthly, enough for her to feel sexually fulfilled.

Fondled From Behind

Kiyoko Shimada, a virgin when she married at twenty-four, was now a woman in her early thirties. She'd known no man other than her husband. The position she liked the most was the one in which she faced frontwards, because her back was the most sensitive part of her body. Her husband initially made a pass at her at their first dance together by running his hand along her back as he wedged their legs together. When he whispered in her ear that he wanted her, she surrendered her virginity to him without a struggle. Now she could always achieve a climax if her husband rode her donkey-wise and forcibly fondled the bones of her spine, one by one. Mrs Shimada's husband was also skilled in stimulating her buttocks as she was being mounted, grabbing them roughly and exerting considerable pressure. They only had sex once weekly, but she was perfectly satisfied with his emphasis on quality rather than quantity.

Hips, Knees, and Legs

Miss Chieko Tadokoro, a 23 year-old office worker, admitted to being most sensitive about the hips, which she preferred to be approached gradually from the legs upwards. She fell in love at nineteen with a college student at a summer resort and let him do anything he wanted, but three months later he abandoned her. She then became a hostess out of sheer desperation and was instructed by one of the customers about sex-sensitivity zones from knees to thighs. He took her home one night and did not so much as glance at her as he vigorously massaged the area above her knees, from beginning to end. And in due time he let his fingers creep along the insides of her hips. At first she experienced a ticklish sensation, but gradually she came to feel as if an electric current was coursing through the centre of her body. Finally, her body drenched in perspiration, she giggled in embarrassment. She felt herself being manipulated as if she were in a sleepwalking trance and that night she discovered the meaning of orgasm. Now she was living with a young labourer, nothing to look at but a most considerate lover. First he kissed the insides of her legs; then, inserting her toes in his mouth, he fondled and kissed his way upwards from calves to knees to lips. She loved him for the services he rendered and couldn't bear the thought of parting, confessing that, 'My sex-sensitivity zones seem to be all concentrated in the lower half of my body. I feel nothing in my breasts or anywhere else.'

The Sex Organs

The Institute's researchers discovered that women who listed the clitoris and the vagina alone as sexually sensitive usually had less satisfactory sex lives than women who also had other zones of sex sensation. Most of these were housewives in their late thirties, indicating that the younger Japanese woman educated in post-war Japan places more emphasis on foreplay than does the older and more passive lady reared in a less progressive era. Miss Etsuko Tanaka had had a procession of lovers, seven in all, but she felt that her present arrangement with a married man who worked alongside her in the same dispensary was unusual enough to add to the annals of sexology. He performed cunnilingus on her in a way that gave her indescribable joy, using his fine moustache to stimulate her vagina with wondrous effect. 'He does that voluntarily because he seems to like it. He doesn't adopt the 'sixty-nine' position but instead presses my waist firmly with his hands and ardently uses his mouth and tongue just as if he were eating watermelon. He always keeps this up for about fifteen minutes.' That's how Miss Tanaka described her married lover who, having performed cunnilingus, engaged directly in intercourse.

Institute researchers were surprised by the large number of women who addressed themselves positively to the male and told him how they wanted to be petted and stimulated. They concluded that Japan is adopting Western ways in sex as well as economics, moving towards an age in which the shy image of the geisha is being replaced by the more aggressive female who knows what she wants sexually and sets out to satisfy her wants in no uncertain terms. Miss Yoko, a 22 year-old office worker, always took the initiative, for example, in petting jousts with her fiancé. What she liked most about his body was his neck, especially the nape. She got extremely excited just from seeing it, bluish in tint, when he returned from the barber's, and after an exchange of kisses she'd caress his neck of her own volition. She'd get him excited through her neck kissing, and this would excite her too. While fondling and biting his shoulders, she'd touch his penis and feel her body throb with desire at the touch. To her, sex sensitivity was not something confined to one or two erogenous zones but rather a thing that she felt everywhere, 'drunk with desire'.

Miss Yukari Torii, a 22 year-old bar hostess, also liked to take the initiative in love encounters. She liked to suck the breasts of the male, having three regular lovers and two others on occasion. The men would abandon themselves to being sucked in this way, drawn to her because she looked so physically desirable. She also preferred performing fellatio to having cunnilingus performed on her. 'When men do such things to me, I feel bad – not in a physical sense, but I can't bear it mentally. But with a man wearing a condom, I can perform fellatio with a feeling of complete satisfaction, getting extremely stimulated by his mounting excitement. I feel and am pleased by the thought that men, who are usually such boastful creatures, become so childlike when this is done to them.' In other words, aroused for her meant acting in such a way that she felt superior to the male sex-mate who was being acted upon.

These up-to-date interviews with young Japanese women prove conclusively that most of them do not feel guilt or shame about sex. And very few regret past love affairs, looking to the future and regarding sex as something to be enjoyed. To cast aside or to be cast aside – to them this is but the way of the world, signifying that male and female in a particular instance are incompatible. It's also noteworthy that only a very small number attach moral value to having lost the hymen in premarital sex relations. In fact, most of them no longer felt sexual love for the man to whom they'd offered their virginity; instead, they were drawn to men who were conversationally adept and sexually skilled. There's a sex revolution taking place in Japan, in which women are starting to exploit the male as a springboard for gaining fuller awareness of female sexuality. The prewar attitude that women were passive objects faithful for life to the man who had sex with them first is being cast aside. These women of postwar Japan are very much concerned with how to make enjoyable sexual techniques an integral part of their lives, and they're not going to tolerate men who are boudoir-ignorant or crude. In prewar Japan the sex act was short and unadorned, but now there is a demand for full and leisurely foreplay and mutually enjoyable consummation. To satisfy this demand, women are looking for the men who are sexually adept. Japanese women appear to be adopting the sexual outlook of American women, more sexually active than before, so Japanese men take note! From now on there are going to be increasing demands on you to be love endurable and sexually skilled.

VI. JAPANESE RULES FOR GIRL-WATCHERS

The Japanese search more than we do for sex universals, seeking to find the keys to man-woman relationships that can apply to all. There is no tradition of ladies first in the land of cherry blossoms, geisha, and heavy machinery, and much less Carrie Nation-style interest in liberating the household drudge and the bar appendage. What the young Japanese male and female do want is a sure knowledge of boudoir positions and touch techniques, a knowledge they try to get from the illustrated manuals available by the dozens. The 'certain she for that certain he' philosophy that pervades the romance-oriented West is alien to the Tokyo-Osaka axis, where experience proves there's safety in numbers, with plurality the best teacher. More Japanese now marry for 'love', as they would put it, but family feelings still count and the matchmaker is still in business, albeit in a reduced role. One sharp difference between East and West in post-marital relations is that Japanese men have few 'hang-ups' or pangs of conscience about playing the night circuit while mama stays at home with hubby's uneaten supper meal before her. Pub-crawling with the boys is a time-honoured tradition, usually done on the spur of the moment without bothering to tell the wife in advance. Another tradition hallowed by time is for a man of means to exhibit his affluence in the form of a mistress or geisha, kept discreetly but well. This becomes a love insurance policy, helping to preserve the outer framework of the earlier Confucian-oriented marriage that was semi-arranged. The double standard prevails, though with the influence of the U.S. on Japanese mores its erosion in this heretofore male paradise is inevitable. But let's leave that question to future researchers and get on with our topics for the day, girl-watching and girl-touching *à la Japonais*.

Girl-Watching

Japan is a crowded country, about half as many people as we have squeezed into an area not quite as large as California. So everyone is close to his or her neighbour and the chances for girl-watching are unlimited. We go in a lot for palmistry, as do the Japanese, but they're also interested in reading past a woman's hands, up to her face and down to her body. This approach appeals to men of all ages and classes, and its exponents have one simple object in mind: to provide their male readers with a valid and effective formula for figuring out a woman's passion potential through the application of proven girl-watching techniques. One writer starts with the ears, calling them a barometer of female sensibility. He divides them into five shapes:

He asserts that the orifice of the outer ear provides a clue to the sensitivity and quality of a woman's sex organs. The third illustration, for example, symbolises a famous sex organ that can satisfy any male, for the entrance may be narrow but it is superlatively deep. Women endowed with this kind of sexual make-up can satisfy the male but they find it difficult to achieve ecstasy for themselves. The sexually frigid woman is said to have the fifth ear-shape; it is not only irregular but the indentation of the aperture of the outer ear is wide and shallow. She may have a beautiful face and a bewitching figure, but her luck with men is all bad. If a husband with a beautiful wife still plays the field, it's because he married a woman with such irregularly-shaped and shallow-indented ears. The second ear-shape reveals a highly-sexed woman, who is said to cry out on attaining orgasm and to use this as a special male-satisfying technique. When Japan had its red-light districts, prior to their abolition in 1958, there were many 'hunters' who searched for the woman with this kind of ear.

The indentation of the aperture of the outer ear not only gives the viewer a good idea of the woman's sexual sensitivities but, according to our Eastern observer, there's one other interesting judgement that can be made from ear analysis. When you look at a woman's face from the front, try to draw a horizontal line to the left and right of the tip of the nose. Then you can compare how that line relates to another imaginary line drawn from the tip of one ear to the tip of the other. The three possibilities are:

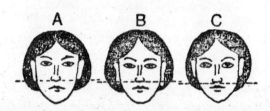

(A) is regarded as the standard, with the lower tips of the ears roughly parallel to the horizontal line that the girl-watcher has drawn from the tip of her nose. (A) is average in sexual interest and sexual stamina. But then there's (B), the woman whose ear tips are lower than the tip of her nose. She's said to have fierce sexual interests and drives, preferring to take the initiative in sex stimulation and body positioning. Having great stamina, normal sexual activity fails to satisfy her. Type (C), on the other hand, finds that the tips of her ears are higher than the tip of her nose. She is not much interested in sex and she tends to be a passive bed-partner. She is demanding in foreplay, with her sexual feelings varying according to room lighting and temperature. Having considered ears and nose, now let's look at the eyes, which are said to reveal a woman's sex life from past to present. Two types of eye areas are delineated,

What do they signify? The 'A' eye is that of a healthy virgin, while the 'B' eye with its many creases belongs to a woman of vast experience. These creases are said to differ somewhat from the creases caused by ageing. The woman who's had excessive sex experience will, according to our analyst, not only have many creases along the lower eyelid but she'll also be yellow-skinned there, no matter how young she is. Now let's proceed from the eye area to the eyes themselves:

 A B C

The 'C' type of eye, in which the pupil inclines towards the top of the eye while the white of the eye is extensive, belongs to a woman with a preference for lesbian love. Chinese face-readers call this type the 'eye with three whites'; women with such eyes are said to have unusual sexual interests, including lesbianism. The woman with an even smaller pupil, the 'B' type, is said to practise self-love, to prefer masturbation to seeking love from a man, and to be more prevalent in England and America than in Japan. She'll have frequent emissions and be fond of using sexual implements. The 'A' type is the most common of the three.

Eyebrows, Hair Under the Armpits

Women with scanty eyebrows have a scant amount of body hair, leading us to conclude that the colour of a woman's eyebrows and the way that they grow are related to hair developments in her abdominal region. Women with thin eyebrows worry about having so few hairs on the rest of their bodies, whereas the woman with thick black eyebrows has so much body hair that she may even irritate her mate's tender skin with it during sexual union. Some Freudian analysts maintain that women with thin eyebrows go for men with thick beards while thick-eyebrowed women fall for beardless men.

Hair quantity is related also to breast size. Women with scant hair under the armpits tend to have small breasts, and women with no hair under their arms generally have such underdeveloped breasts that in appearance they're just like those of the male. They usually feel no sexual sensations when their breasts are stroked,

141

though along the neck and back they're more sexually sensitive than other women.

Mouths Show Degrees of Love Fickleness

In the East, from antiquity onwards the resemblance of mouth shape and vagina shape was noted and sexually associated. Face-readers believe that the mouth reveals recent concerns and desires, sex experiences past and present, and sexuality now and to be. Women who naturally adopt an open-mouthed pose or seem weak-lipped are highly sexed, as are women whose lower lips are moist.

The Large-Mouthed – A Dangerous Type

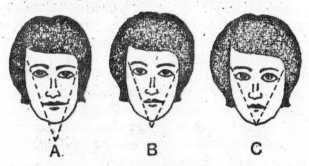

A.   B   C

The way for girl-watchers to judge mouth shapes is for them to draw a straight (imaginary, of course!) line from the outer end of each eye to the corresponding corners of the mouth. Then note where the lines would meet were they to be extended, as in the drawings above. (B) is a fairly common type, (A) the type associated with large-mouthed women. Women with (B) mouth types tend towards introversion and are reticent about plunging into love affairs. But they often find compassion developing into love. They get involved in relations with married men and are victimised in love triangles. A woman with the (A) type mouth will be vigorous in movement, more of a doer than a thinker. She often repents later of the mistakes she makes through impetuosity but she'll make the same mistakes again and again. She likes young love partners and attracts weak-willed men. Passive women tend to have the (C) type mouth, with the imaginary lines drawn from eye corners to mouth corners coming to a point within the chin area. They seem disinterested in sex but they can become strongly attached and to more than one man. They easily become Number

Two Wives in Japan. and as bar hostesses they may not be the prettiest but they will be the ones most in demand.

Chin and Forehead,
or How to Size Up a Woman at a Glance

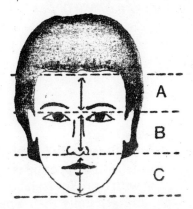

If you want to size up a woman at a glance, and your time is limited, start with her chin. If you're sitting opposite her, look at her chin and forehead and do a threefold visual measurement. In other words, as our illustration shows, measure the part of her face above her eyes, the part from the tip of her eyes to the tip of her nose, and then glance from the tip of her nose to the tip of her chin. You'll generally find three types:

1. Forehead and chin almost equal in length
2. Chin longer than forehead
3. Forehead longer than chin

How do these types differ? Type one represents the woman easily addicted to romantic daydreams, the woman drawn to mood and repelled by material considerations. She'll comply if the mood is right, even though her conscience dictates otherwise, and she loves to be led down the primrose path of scenic beauty and high adventure. The second type, chin-longer-than-forehead, is more down to earth; love and marriage to her are closely linked terms. She's strong spirited and prefers diamonds to daydreams. Strongly compassionate, she's drawn to weak men who crave maternal handling, and she'll easily offer up her love to only sons and to orphans. She's hard to capture, but once ensnared she becomes sexually forward and transformed. The third type (forehead longer than chin) is prone to hysteria, vain and excessively proud of her talents, beauty, and lineage. She is very status-conscious, with strong but hidden sex desires. Persistence wins this woman, who'll say she dislikes sex while making it apparent that she enjoys it to the utmost.

Lastly, the Lips of a Strongly-Sexed Woman

Look at her face slightly from the side. In (A), the upper and lower lip are equally thick, while in (B) the upper lip is somewhat thinner than the lower lip. Women with lips like (A) tend to be more highly sexed than the (B) type, and generally their upper lips protrude slightly forward. Two lines may also clearly protrude between the lower part of the nose and the upper lip. A woman with such protruding lines may look weak but she's a sex dynamo. When the lines appear parallel to the lips instead of at right angles to them, it means that the woman can't be satisfied by one man alone; the lines are said to reveal the force of her lascivious desires.

Girl-Watchers of the world! Use this analysis the next time you're killing time in a crowded bus or department store; you have nothing to lose but your minds!

For the first time in paperback—an intriguing and informative look at sex and love in the mysterious Orient.

"The Japanese male has kept woman down to earth and in easy reach of his beck and call. To exult or idealise her was considered unmanly, unbecoming and un-Japanese."